T0146591

Experience Life Through the Passage of Spirit

JOURNEY BEYOND LINEAR TIME

Raphael Jara

BALBOA.
PRESS
A DIVISION OF HAY HOUSE

The information in this book is at all times restricted to education, teaching, and training on the subject of holistic, spiritual living and does not involve diagnosing of mental, spiritual, or physical health issues.

Balboa Press books may be ordered through booksellers or by contacting:

Balboa Press
A Division of Hay House
1663 Liberty Drive
Bloomington, IN 47403
www.balboapress.com
1 (877) 407-4847

Because of the dynamic nature of the Internet, any web addresses or links contained in this book may have changed since publication and may no longer be valid. The views expressed in this work are solely those of the author and do not necessarily reflect the views of the publisher, and the publisher hereby disclaims any responsibility for them.

The author of this book does not dispense medical advice or prescribe the use of any technique as a form of treatment for physical, emotional, or medical problems without the advice of a physician, either directly or indirectly. The intent of the author is only to offer information of a general nature to help you in your quest for emotional and spiritual well-being. In the event you use any of the information in this book for yourself, which is your constitutional right, the author and the publisher assume no responsibility for your actions.

Any people depicted in stock imagery provided by Thinkstock are models, and such images are being used for illustrative purposes only. Certain stock imagery © Thinkstock.

Print information available on the last page.

ISBN: 978-1-5043-6685-4 (sc)
ISBN: 978-1-5043-6686-1 (hc)
ISBN: 978-1-5043-6702-8 (e)

Library of Congress Control Number: 2016915683

Balboa Press rev. date: 11/21/2016

Contents

Contents

Acknowledgments

While there are many people who have inspired me, four have truly made a deep impact on my life.

I wish to acknowledge my daughter Leeya, who at the age of three surprised me deeply for the first time, although there were many more surprises to come. While driving home one afternoon, a conversation ensued about love: the loss of love, what is true love, and the dynamics of keeping love fresh and pure so that it can last. Suddenly, I realized that I was having a very intelligent, adult conversation with a three-year-old! I hurriedly pulled the car over to the side of the road, looked into her eyes, and asked, "Who are you? There is something inside you with a greater mind than that of a child." A mysterious smile appeared on her face. She was aware that I understood. I therefore want to acknowledge all children who have incarnated on this planet within the last twenty-five years, who brought with them a higher mind and a deep will for change to assist humanity in an upward shift.

And the following female friends have illumined the path of my spiritual journey:

- Josephine Auciello, who was the first to enlighten me on the fact that I had "mommy issues," and she was instrumental in setting the tone for how to release the wound and the memory and to become free of them. This has brought about tremendous knowledge and wisdom about what we carry inside our energy field, how the baggage is formed, and their purpose for our evolution.
- Jodie Lobana, the enlightened one that carries so much grace and poise. She lives in complete freedom and ease and sees the light

in everyone and everything. Our conversations are deep and pure and are always revelatory to us both.

- Marilyn Siou. It is through the eyes of this beautiful princess that I saw up close and personal the light of the soul. It is through this bond that I have recognized that love without conditions is the only true love there is. And true love will never dim, not in this lifetime or in the ones to come.

Author's Note

I suspect that the greatest misconception that most people hold in their hearts and minds is that they are mere humans. And wherever the heart and mind go, we go with them. This belief of being mere humans is the beginning of our bondage here on earth. If we believe that we are merely this human body, then we have limited ourselves to a reality that says we are born, we die, and that's all there is. Holding this mind-set further states that we are locked into the confines of earth, limited only to earthly experiences, thinking we have no effect on the human race. Furthermore, it blocks any awareness of our ability to access higher dimensions, our ability to find our true self, our ability to make full use of the breadth and depth of mind, and our ability to accomplish extraordinary things.

But furthermore, if we believe we are limited, what would be the point of this everlasting and continuous biorhythm called life, if we can only indulge in it for eighty years, which is a mere blip in time? Who then is life for, and what would be the point of perpetuity? Who is it then that explores the vastness of this ever-expanding universe if there is no one to garner the experiences?

The most brilliant minds on earth, past and present, broke through the barriers of earthly confines to attain new knowledge relative to science and technology, as well as fresh new approaches to life and living. This book attempts to splinter any beliefs of limitation, for we are the universe - a continuous unified ground in a single universal field of existence and intelligence. We are the expressions of the universal self. We are universal consciousness. There is no other. We come to earth cloaked in a human body. We come as the many, but we are a single organism that must function as one as we co-create life and the future together. Thusly, we are bound together through time and space. In this book, I share some of my experiences with you so that you can see that there are no limits to the things that can be achieved when you move deeper into the light of your true self. And these experiences transcend time and space. You will learn that love itself, the nature of the soul, also transcends time and space. You will learn that we are not bound by the proclivities of earth, for a deeper truth is that the universe is our playground.

I hope I have done this book justice in allowing you to easily assimilate the information and earnestly apply it, and then live it. This book is a roadmap that lights the path on the spiritual journey from the beginning and moves you towards merging with your higher self, also called soul ascension or enlightenment. The objective is to become a different person with higher spiritual vibrations, to become detached from the bondage that placates this place and let go of egotistic patterns to see truth more clearly. You will experience the prevalent oneness that *is* humanity and understand the deeper intricacies of this life we all share.

I thank you from my heart for reading this book. And may peace be with you as you gain the knowledge of your true self and spread the seeds of the gifts you came here to express for the benefit of the many.

Introduction

I feel especially lucky, for my life has been exceedingly interesting. Yes, there were ups and downs and sideways, all relative to our physical anchor here on earth—relative to the things we unconsciously hold dear in mind and the baggage we unknowingly carry when we don't know who we truly are and what we are doing here on earth. But we are far more than our personalities and our engrained or self-created beliefs. We are complex beings living in the physical world and the spirit world all at once. And when we become aware of this, our awareness and our life takes on a whole new meaning. Our perspective will shift to accommodate our broader awareness, bringing us deeper insights into life and ourselves. We gain insight into the true nature of all things and begin to experience truths as life unfolds through us.

How do I know this? I have walked on this earth on two occasions in pure spirit, while still in a human body. I am not referring to previous incarnations but in the here and now, between the years 2011 and 2013. The energy vibrating through me was constant and steady and felt very much like high-voltage electricity percolating through me from the inside out, but with lightness to its vibration, which enabled me to feel as if I could float. I knew that the light emitting from my being may not be seen by others, but it most certainly could be felt.

In the first instance, I became aware that if I had gone to the park, the birds and the squirrels would come, the dogs would come, the trees would feel my awareness and I would feel theirs, and young children would sense the light and feel an obligation to move toward it. In the second instance, I was on a subway and could see inside others, not with my eyes but with a deep awareness, a higher knowing. I could see and feel their assortments of pain, guilt, shame, and all other words that describe the wounds we carry around with us. This is our unseen and untold baggage that dims our experiences of the wonders of life. I understood that when we take the time to heal our psychological wounds, a purity of spirit unfolds from within—an aliveness, a unity—resulting in a broader state of being. Herein, we begin to experience freedom.

I have also been fortunate to know the qualities of the soul through a series of subtle experiences. These are experiences in which the soul becomes functionally present and the body and mind become the observers, being pulled into the current of the phenomenon as it unfolds. The validity of these experiences remains in the body and mind such that they become aware that observable facts can happen beyond their doing or understanding. However, the body and mind are quickly updated so they too evolve.

Our physical body is nailed to the earth's atmosphere, but we are spirit, and spirit is unencumbered by boundaries. Once we return to the light, we have no limits and no boundaries, even while wearing a human body. We transcend all of it.

As we learn and grow from the knowledge that we are spirit, life becomes an adventure. We realize that we are connected to the universal self, the master orchestrator of our life. And our movement with life happens according to its will. We learn that the experiences we face are for our good, and we must look earnestly for the treasures within them.

In recent years, many souls are turning toward spiritual awareness. They intuitively realize that there must be more to life than what they have previously thought. There is a knowing in them that there is a deeper state of being through which they can begin to truly know themselves, their purpose, and this one life to a much greater degree. Some of the profound questions that arise in their search for knowledge are these: Why are we here? Why do we suffer? How do we find ourselves? Where is God?

This book illuminates the path to help the reader on his or her journey and move the unconscious mind into a state of higher consciousness. It removes the mental strain of trying to ascertain what should be done to heighten your vibration, and it acknowledges the baggage and the wounds to be understood and released in order to gain wisdom, allowing us to truly become God's vehicle here on earth.

Allow me to explain what I mean by baggage.

There once was a man who wanted guidance to resolve his problems and find real happiness. He decided to go on a pilgrimage to seek the wisdom of a well-known enlightened master. The enlightened master lived at the very top of one of the mountains in the Himalayas. The man knew the journey would be arduous, but he felt desperate to find solutions to what ailed him.

On his climb up the mountain, he became overwhelmed by the journey. He was facing extreme cold weather, altitude sickness, and pure exhaustion. His mind became his worst enemy, filling his head with doubt for taking on such a climb. Fear took him over as well. "Will I make it alive?" "Will this great sage really help me?" He could see where the sage was on top of the mountain but wasn't sure if he was going to make it. He collapsed in utter despair about the situation.

Being omniscient, the master knew of this man's ordeals. He left his simple hut and walked to the edge of the mountain. Seeing the man sitting hunched in the snow, he yelled in a loud voice, "Let go of your baggage and your climb will be much easier!"

Startled, the man looked up the mountain to see the master standing there laughing at his situation. Confused at first by the sage's command, the man realized it had nothing to do with the physical baggage he carried for his survival but the mental and emotional baggage he was holding on to. With this awareness, the man rose to his feet and continued with the climb, releasing the fears and doubts that plagued him as he went along the mountain.

When he reached the top, the master welcomed him with open arms and took him into his hut for warmth and tea. No words passed between them for a very long time, but the seeker felt lighter and happier. He felt there was nothing to ask for. He felt complete within himself.

With the glint of divine knowledge in his wise eyes, finally the master asked, "why did you come to see me?" Searching his mind and heart, the seeker said, "Nothing, master. I feel complete."

"Good! Good! Take rest and meditate, and tomorrow, be on your way," replied the master. The seeker followed the master's command, even though he had never meditated before. He went to the farthest corner of the hut, where a small straw mat lay, and sat on it. Without effort, he fell into a deep state of meditation. When he came out of meditation, he saw that it was early the next morning as the sun began to rise over the mountains. The master presented him with more tea, which he gladly accepted. He felt transformed with a greater sense of himself—his God self. He felt pure and humbled by his experience.

He was told, before his journey, that it is always wise to leave an offering to show gratitude for all that he received from the master. As he was about to leave the hut for his journey down the mountain, he opened his travel bag and withdrew a small pouch of coins. He then bowed and presented the pouch to the master, quietly thanking him for all that he received. He did this knowing that what he offered would never be enough for what he received. The master took the pouch and smiled without saying a word and the seeker took his leave.

The book starts with shining a light on fear, since fear is the greatest barrier to human expansion and evolution. Once fear is understood and put in its rightful place, a tremendous load will be lifted, which will be felt in body, in the mind, and in one's state of being. Mind itself has become aligned with heaps of rubbish that we consistently create and carry around with us, the weight of which leaves most of us feeling completely lost at times. For some, this weight remains in their mind for most of their lives, yet all of it is unnecessary. Chapter 2 addresses how to remove conflicts and debris and all the fragmented noise from the mind, thus allowing space to think, to breathe, to be, and to grow. Now it's time to find yourself, who you truly are—not from the fragments of your so-called personality, but from the depths of your being. Meditation assists you in finding your true self, and you learn to embrace who you are without blame and without self-criticism. A deeper meditation takes you into the void, a state of being where you truly realize your formlessness, your essence, and your connection to all there is. This is sobering, because for the first time in your physical life, you will realize that you are beyond the physical, that you are an infinite being of light and that humanity is but one single unified force, co-creating life together in this universal field of existence. With this knowing, you will look at others differently. You will begin to understand that all are but one, cloaked behind superficial differences of race, language, country of origin, and culture. Thus is the paradox of duality.

Through deeper meditation, you begin to lighten your load and gain broader awareness. You learn that you are pure consciousness, consciousness is the observer, and the observer informs you through self-awareness. Thusly, you begin to teach yourself on a deeper level, from the inside out. You further learn how to still the mind, allowing your intuition to be heard, felt, and acknowledged. In this frame of mind, you begin to recognize more of who you are from the inside and know that the more space the mind has, the more aware you become of yourself and of life. Wisdom is being formed in you, as you are being released from the bondage of the mind. You are becoming free.

You will learn that you are a system of energy living in the physical and spiritual worlds all at once. This system of energy contains the attributes of who you are as spirit, including your thoughts, your emotions, and your mind. It is within the spiritual bodies that your subconscious mind resides, which carries the contents of your childhood wounds and houses the karma you created in this life and in previous incarnations. All this must be healed, for the healing releases the burden and weight you have been carrying and creates productive energy, which brings lightness. You move to a higher state of consciousness, your awareness deepens, your wisdom multiplies, and your mind and body are freed and relaxed. This heightens your spiritual vibration and life becomes easier. You are evolving. If you remain faithful through the healing process and learn how to manage your emotional well-being so as not to reintroduce additional baggage into your energy system, you will mature into deeper aspects of the mind. Your intelligence and brainpower will increase and your mental strain will lessen.

Your inner child stands at the doorway to your highest evolution, but worry not. Chapter 6 teaches you how to heal the inner child absolutely. As your consciousness and knowledge of your energy system improves, you will learn that your wounds are your calling. They prepare you for aspects of yourself and life that you came here to impart to humanity for the healing of the whole. You will gain deeper knowledge of yourself as you learn how to heal others through speaking, touching, writing, and other means of assisting others, including being present in your own powerful energy field. You learn to further clear the path to your soul through yoga and pranayama—the breath. You will understand that what you see simply as the air you breathe is actually cosmic energy, prana—a universal creative force that is spirit. It is the God energy in and around us. And when it moves through the body with focused intention, it resolves anything inside the body that is not in harmony with the fullness of the body and mind. It removes diseases, stresses, unproductive traits and habits, and negative mind state. It removes, fears and compulsions and it removes your karma while endowing you with a youthful glow. Your body and mind become more powerful from the inside. Yoga/pranayama cleanses you completely and readies your body and mind to merge with the soul.

Chapter 9 brings you to the task of liberating the soul. That is, releasing you from earth's mental bondage. You now see life as it is, without presuppositions and mindless beliefs. You will learn to rid the ego while moving deeper into the mind of the soul. You will learn how to move steadfastly along the continuum of the soul, refining yourself, your habits, and your motives and using your abilities for the sake of humanity. As your spiritual vibration increases, you will begin to experience the subtleties of spirit, taking you beyond linear time, and you will know that you are becoming one with the light of your being. You are merging with the soul.

This book, in its sequential form and with the exercises provided, will bring you to a deeper knowledge of truth, which will raise your level of consciousness. Through higher consciousness, you will be guided to your own divine experiences here on earth. Through these experiences, you are touching the Absolute and will recognize that you and the Absolute are one and the same. You will wonder no further about whether or not divinity exists. You will know that you are a cog in this single unified field of existence. And for humanity, you will know that "the one is the many" and "the one" can touch "the many" by becoming aligned with his or her true nature, which is the nature of the soul. Namaste.

An Intuitive Mind

Some years ago, I picked up an acorn in a park, and when I reached home, I pulled up an image of a mature oak tree on my Mac computer. It was captivating to look upon the massive and expansive oak tree, which seems to have poise all to itself. I reflected on the contrast between the seed and the finished product: a fully-grown mature tree of immense stature. It occurred to me that if a tree can expand itself to such breadth, depth, and magnificence, why not man? For we also carry a seed within from which we can mold ourselves into the deep desires that are entrenched within our hearts. We have the real potential to express and expand ourselves into our greatest desires, touching the hearts of the many in a state of grace. Our only limit is our self, for one who knows himself or herself from within has no limits or restrictions. Through the force of our desires, any goal to which we aspire can be attained, for we hold the power of spirit within.

I was guided to write this book many months before I actually succumbed to writing it. There were ripples in the air around and within me—an undulating urge to write. I had always known the time would come, so I pondered for a few weeks on what subject I could write. I was aware that the subject would have to be of significant value to humanity in the here and now, but nothing came. So one day, I spoke out loud. "I know that you want me to write, but on what subject?" I placed those words upon the wind and rested. Some months later, my business lost a significant amount of funds in two very uncanny and bizarre circumstances, occurring only three months apart, thus bringing the business to an abrupt end. Several months later, I had to give up my condo, and with no new income in sight,

I landed in a room in a basement—just me with four walls, quietude, and the wonder of how I got there. On the third morning, there was movement. The book began to percolate through me, taking form inside my awareness. One could say the book wrote itself through me. There is a shallow void that exists between being asleep and being awake. We pass through this void every morning on our way to becoming fully awake. In that shallow empty opening is a sacred space of no mind in which we rest as our divine self for a moment. It was in this space that I began to receive the information and the flow you are now reading.

The book arrived when all my distractions were gone, when all that remained was surrender. The ritual every morning was writing fast enough on blank sheets of paper to keep up with the information flooding through me. The information continued to flow as I arose from my bed and moved to the computer. During the daytime, when I was able to affix my awareness in the silent space, the information continued to flow. I didn't need to ask where this information was coming from, because as you read this book, you will know that I have been somewhat spiritually awake my whole life. For you, this writing will identify a practical sequence of knowledge to be acquired and realizations to encounter in order to return to the knowing of who you truly are. There is much more to life than meets the eye.

We didn't incarnate on this planet to simply go to school, make money, buy a house, get married, have children, battle many of life's problems, and then grow old and wither away. There is more to life than we suspect. Soul comes to earth cloaked in a human body, and its journey is deliberate. As you will read in Chapter 9, soul carries inside its energy field an altruistic longing to return into the light from whence it came. A part of its journey on earth is one of remembrance of its true source, its true nature, and calling. Every man and woman on this planet feels this pull, but most simply ignore it in order to remain inside the flow of human frailty.

Man is God's vehicle on earth, and God experiences life through man. But man must first put his human frailty aside and follow his divine calling. And to do this requires great courage and determination. It requires you to undo the rubble you have created through simple mind and rebuild yourself from divine light from the inside out. It requires living in a state of grace while remaining unaffected by what most on this planet do or how they live. This requires steadfastness, humility, and every ounce of willpower one carries. This is the true life. Your awareness will lead the way. Awareness is a knowing—an instinctive, conscious knowing. When you become aligned with it, your life will move to a higher state of being, a deeper level of knowing, and a broader perspective on life will ensue. This will bring you to truth and not the illusions that appease the unconscious mind. The beginning of awareness positions you on the journey of your true self. You will gain experiences, subtle experiences that are magical in nature revealing things that you would consider out of this world. You will know through these experiences that you are not simple but rather that you are a being of immense potential. You will begin to understand your abilities and your legacy, which is what you came here to deliver to humanity. As your awareness becomes broader, many more things will reveal themselves to you and your subtle experiences will become deeper, more profound. You will be moving systematically out of a shallow illusionary frame of mind and into a broader perspective of this one life toward knowing your true self.

Throughout this book, I share some of my own divine experiences with you in hopes that you will know what lives within you and within all of us. Heaven is not *out there*, nor is it *up there* somewhere. It is right here, right now, where we stand. When we continue to raise our level of awareness, deeper insights and revelations will ensue, for they must to allow us to gain a higher level of consciousness and know who we are in the here and now. Our newfound knowledge, wisdom, and subtle experiences will lead the way to a new realization and a very different state of being. The life we lead will take us to the center of the universe, where we will know that we are bound by no thing, for the universe is our playground. This book, in its ideal sequencing, is your pointer for a far more sacred life on planet Earth.

My Youth Sprung Forth Wisdom

My remembrance of my life began at the age of twelve. I don't remember much of myself prior to that age, but I remember and acknowledge everything from twelve up to the present. It has been a fantastic ride, and by that I mean aspects of my life as it unfolded held a promise of direction, growth, and the realizations that would take me to where I now stand.

Know that nothing that happens in our lives—what we refer to as problems—is hurled at us to harm us. There are no accidents, no matter how ill fated any circumstance may look. Our lives are orchestrated to take us directly to where we must be and to know who we must become. At the tender age of thirteen, I had the awareness that one day I would write, speak, and demonstrate through experiences that this life we share is the only life there is. This knowledge would benefit humankind. I became consciously aware that I did not come from this place we call Earth, but I came to Earth for a reason. I also sensed that those around me, including my family and my peers, did not have this realization of themselves, so I felt almost out of place, a one-off from others. It was quite a challenge for a young boy to reconcile, so I chose to just remain constantly aware. The state we call human consciousness, that state most fall into unconsciously during their childhood years, was not a part of my makeup. Many things that interested others were of no interest to me; the things that drew my interest were of little or no interest to others. As time went on, my differences became more apparent, both to me and to others. I had abilities with mind. I mean, mind would bring me insights into things, giving me the ability to solve problems or complex situations. Mind would give me creative insights when needed for a given situation, and wisdom—yes, wisdom—when faced with situations that required a higher mind. My abilities included solving people problems, situational problems, or abstract problems. I could see the missing links in things and the broken pieces in processes, procedures, or the like. To this end, I spent much of my idle time inventing new products in thought and principle only, products that should be readily available but were not. Over the years, I watched as these products were introduced into the marketplace through others who had the financial means and support to develop and market them.

Whenever a problem arose among others (within my earshot), the wisdom required to squash the problem would arrive in my mind, either in the form of a solution or in the form of an insight. The insight might be that neither party was listening to the other. And I would ask them to take turns truly listening to each other. Problems are typically solved when both sides are heard and understood. My peers were perplexed because I was one of them, yet I could see and solve things they could barely understand. I felt a sense of foreboding from the realization that they felt that I was not one of them after all. I was standing in reach and power of mind and knew that this would serve the purpose for which I had come to earth in this incarnation. I did not ask, "Why me?" There was an awareness that the reason would reveal itself in due time.

I was shy, possibly from the hesitance to speak—not wanting to be looked at as if I was an alien. But I learned and understood things quickly and accurately. I excelled very quickly in the classroom, and in a broad range of sports. I did not study or try to memorize things, because it seemed that my brain and mind would open up when I needed them—as if all the answers were resting inside my frontal lobe. My memory of things I learned was exceptional. For example, I could read a passage in a book and recite the entire passage perfectly weeks or even months later. Therefore, I floated through middle school and high school, skipping some grades, and landed in university at an early age.

Outside school, things were the same. I recalled the first incident that attracted adults to my abilities. I had overheard an argument between the parents of one of my friends. I don't recall the crux of the argument, but I do remember that the solution relative to their woes came to me in a vivid and clear form. I relayed the message to my friend and advised him to share it with his parents. They were shocked. It was the answer they could not see for themselves. They began to call on me frequently to help them solve other issues and to help clarify things for their decision-making. Through word of mouth, other married couples and single adults began calling on me to solve all kinds of issues for them. Solving adult problems had me feeling a bit out of place—too much information for a young man's ears. So at some point, I purposefully became very difficult to find, bringing the therapy sessions to a close.

My two sisters, my mother, and I arrived in Canada when I was sixteen years old. I quickly developed friendships with others with whom I felt a connection, those with similarities in character and interest in the sports I loved to play. By this time, I had developed an even deeper awareness of my mental capabilities. I kept my solutions to myself for the most part, for fear that they may not be understood by others. However, there were times when I had to let it out, especially in situations where I felt some discussions could potentially turn hostile, due to a lack of understanding in one or both parties. It was amazing to me that others could only see and believe their own point of view, and in that frame of mind, problems that exist could never be fully seen, understood, or solved. So again I played the rescuer. Some understood the solution immediately, and others were perplexed. I have had friends tell me four years after I delivered a solution that they did not understand it then but now they do. I gained respect from friends. They did not ask how I knew these things. They were just happy that I was in their circle. I became the unwilling go-to guy in a sense—the reluctant leader of the pack.

Here I was in the middle of my teenage development and finally feeling a unity with my abilities and myself. My friends wanted to do things that most teenagers wanted to do for pleasure, to challenge themselves, or to try and find themselves. Some of these things were slightly dangerous, some were unhealthy, and others were absolutely ridiculous. I, however, did not indulge. My interests were different. Where they wanted to constantly discuss football and hockey games, I played and excelled in many sports instead. I was always interested in doing, and not in frivolous chatter. And when my friends wanted to go to the mall to hang out, I went home and read more about the human condition or practiced my tae kwon do on the wall or on my mother's curtains. When they wanted to talk about girls, well, that subject interested me quite a bit, because I loved the feminine form and energy. I suspect though that I skipped the teenage rebellious stage, for I had always felt more mature than my teenage counterparts. I was not bored. My curiosity about life was an itch that needed to be scratched. I wanted to know the psychology of man and the psychology of our planet. I wanted to know what drove people—both those who reached for success and those who seemed aimless. I wanted to know if an aimless person could be transformed into a productive person, and if so, how? I wanted to know what is mind, for I instinctually knew that mind did not live inside the brain. My own mind seemed impetuous and could get me information even when I did not ask for it, at least not consciously. So at around age seventeen, I started the search for answers. I started with Sigmund Freud and moved on to Robert Blake. I looked for anyone who was an authority on human psychology and on mind. In the 1970s, there was not much information on mind, perhaps because man and science had not yet ascertained what "mind" is. However, I did locate a book called *Science of Mind*, which spoke very scantily about mind.

Needless to say, I stayed within my own form. I was not swayed away from the things that interested me most, no matter how strong a pull my friends exerted. I felt an inner depth that was unshakeable. I followed my own path then, and that is true even to this day. For example, I still have little interest in getting together with others to drink and chat on frivolous matters. But when there are conversations with a purpose, to solve problems or to pull apart the mysteries of things, I am interested.

I remained in a state of awareness, of myself, of others, and of life in general. At age eighteen, I had gained an understanding of the things that touched my heart and formed desires in me. I became aware that the deep desires that rest in us were not cultivated by external forces. They just arrive from within and are felt in the heart to get our attention. They are the roadmap for our journey. I had seen many homeless people in this rich country of Canada, living and dying on the streets, and it seemed that the government was doing very little about it. Yet here I was with a myriad of solutions at my fingertips. I saw fourteen-year-old girls selling their bodies on the streets in downtown Toronto, being controlled and bullied by pimps. I became familiar with the injustice being expelled on people of color. They were not readily hired for jobs they were qualified for or they were kept out of certain positions within companies and paid less than their counterparts. I have seen police targeting young black males in an attempt to harass them and keep them feeling frightened. In fact, I experienced it myself between the ages of sixteen and nineteen. My awareness was that the police wanted young black males to know that police were the ones in control and that they had the power—a tactic of gross intimidation. They could intentionally harass black youths with the knowledge that the system of which they are a part was on their side.

This was my first time having racism pointed at me. And this was interesting to me, because I am Jamaican born and Jamaica is a nation that has a collection of all races of people from across the world. I saw no racism there. In fact, all those who live in Jamaica—whether they are African, German, Chinese, Japanese, Russian, Portuguese, Latin, Indian, or all the other nations of people that have lived there for generations—call themselves Jamaican. They speak the dialect; they relate to each other in a way that portrays oneness; they share and laugh together, because they are together as one heart of the nation. The motto that encapsulates the ideal of this small island is "Out of many, one people." This tells me that, as a whole, the nation represents and understands humanity—a unit of one functioning as the many. So for me, any premise outside of oneness was fallacious.

At nineteen, I made a decision that I wanted to be wealthy. Although my purpose for being here on earth was not totally clear, I felt that a part of my fellowship with life was to level the playing field for those who were unfortunate and those who were being held back. I intended to spread wealth so that others could be in a place of abundance and choice, where they could realize their own potential, versus being in a place of lack. By twenty-five, I had amassed wealth across several modes of investments, including real estate, retail, stocks, and mutual funds. I had developed several businesses, which included a retail store in Yorkville, the richest shopping district in Toronto. All this, while I systematically climbed the corporate ladder in the field of information technology, my chosen career in the data center at one of Canada's major banks.

If what I achieved seems impossible, know that everything becomes possible when you hold an unshakeable state of mind that nothing will stop you from achieving what you desire. Are your desires from the heart? Are they for the good of yourself and others? Are your motives pure? Then be bold in expanding and expressing yourself, for the ground on which you stand is solid.

The Barrier of Fear

Fears are hypnotic in nature, allowing some to give up on their dreams and desires, thus binding themselves to mediocrity. Know that all fears can be released, thus leaving room for abundant productive energies. Let's examine the destructive patterns of fear when allowed to roam unencumbered inside the psyche of man.

Fear is the greatest threat to ail the human psyche from expanding into the fullness of life. Fear is the holder and keeper of the simple mind. It takes refuge in the ego mind, crippling most from ever realizing their own true identify or from expanding into the limitless possibilities of their true potential. From those who have journeyed back from the grip of death, who have seen the truth and the light from where we came, their fervent message to humanity is to *fear nothing!*

Fear holds you fastidiously in a state of illusion, of not knowing, yet always reaching, searching for what is true, what is real. You are always floating like an autumn leaf in the wind, never really knowing who you are, your full capabilities, or how to foster creativity and brilliance consistently in all you do. Most believe themselves to be the attributes of their so-called personality. The problem is that personalities are mind constructs created by the ego mind, which is festered in fear and doubt. Anything that is fear based is ineffective and can only lead you deeper into the prison of simple mind. Do not rely on your personality as verification of who you are. The attributes of personality are fleeting—there one day, gone in a month. But know this: who we truly are is permanent and substantive and wields incredible power and potential for growth, both for our self and for humanity.

Fear of Advancements

When it comes to moving ahead, particularly in your career or job, fear becomes your friend. Fear tells you that there are aspects of your next move for which you have little or no experience or education. Or fear may have you procrastinate, wanting things to be perfect before you act. Then after taking action, fear either gives you stress over being perfect or tells you that you will fail or—even worse—that you will succeed. You derail yourself and the opportunities. The best thing to do is assess the situation carefully. If it is true that the adventure you are embarking on is new for you, or if there are aspects you are unfamiliar with, don't worry. You can become well practiced or educated in the areas you are lacking. You can also enroll someone who already has the skills to assist you by joining your team.

At age twenty-one, I had read J. Paul Getty's book on real estate investments and had decided to pursue this avenue at some point. I had no real experience whatsoever. One day, I overheard a coworker speaking to a real estate agent on his phone. He was roughly forty-five years old and had recently joined the technical team in the data center. At that time, the data center had amassed many recent university grads, most around the age of twenty-two, including myself at age twenty-one. I sat with him and asked about his real estate experience. He told me that he owned many rental properties across the city and had been doing this for over twenty years. So right there, on the spot, I made him an offer. I told him that if he could show me how to get started in real estate wisely, I would teach him the ins and outs of our complex operating system, which would significantly elevate his problem-solving techniques and abilities. He said yes, and we shook hands. "So where do I start?" I asked him. He told me to get $5,000 and he would introduce me to his real estate agent.

Once I put my mind to something, there is no turning back, and time is always of the essence with me, so in two months, I had put aside $5,000 and off we went to meet his real estate agent. Keep in mind that this was 1982. Today, you are required 20 percent as a down payment, so $5,000 down today would only work if you were purchasing a shack. I purchased my first property two days later, and it felt really good.

Once settled, I hired a friend to do minor renovations to freshen the look and the vibe of the place. Then I asked the agent to come over and give advice on the effects of the renovation, and things took an unusual turn. He was quite impressed at how fresh and well done the place looked after the renovation. He said that I could make a substantial profit if I sold it now. I pondered only for a moment and then said yes. I sold the property without regret and received a profit more substantial than he had suggested. I then purchased a larger condo suite in which to live. Over the following years, I continued to purchase and hold rental properties, as well as other properties that were renovated and resold. I had created a dual cash flow, which was significant for building wealth. Having two streams of income from my fresh start in the real estate business was promising. I loved the art of renovating, creating spaces with pristine overtures. Ten years later, I went back to school and acquired an advanced certification in architecture. I formed my own company in 2003 to produce exceptionally designed homes with a more natural flow throughout, encompassing features and finishing that were esthetically pleasing and producing an air of serenity. This was the business I lost in 2013 while being nudged to write this book. The end of one thing always leads to the beginning of something else if we avoid fear and remain in the awareness.

Starting my retail store was a similar endeavor. I had a burning desire to bring beautiful art pieces in crystal and glass, made by the world's most prominent glass blowers, to the Toronto marketplace. However I had no experience in retail. That did not frighten me, because I understood that I needed to learn the game of retail. I had a strong belief in my abilities to excel, beyond what I learned in a book or in a classroom, using creativity and insights from my own mental capabilities. I knew Hazelton Lanes, a shopping district for the wealthy, would be the right place for the products. So again, I asked for help. The first person I asked to help was my girlfriend. She was brilliant with accounting and was overall very bright. She said yes.

This yes was more important than I realized at the time, for over the years to come, the realization sank in that having a devoted commitment and support from my lover and partner was substantive. I realized that love and support from the feminine can send a man to higher heights than he could have fostered for himself. There is something quite relenting and deep when the male and female energies are bound together in support and harmony: miracles can come of it. But that's another book.

So off we went to the trade show in Frankfurt, Germany—the largest trade show on the planet at that time. We met many suppliers with extraordinary products, and during dinner with one of them, we advised him that we had no practical retail experience. He suggested he would help, and he did. In fact, he flew from Los Angeles to Toronto the day prior to our opening and helped us with proper organization of the items in the store. He said there was a psychology to how things are presented in order to appeal to those in eyeshot. He always remained open to helping us and offering his advice. He asked for nothing in return and was just happy to see such a young couple being so inspired. He said we reminded him of himself and his wife twenty years earlier.

Inspiration drives people. Inspiration also motivates others to grant you the help you need.

The message here is this: Don't spend your time feeling afraid to move forward with your plans. There are many who would love to help. Simply ask.

In some cases, you can offer a position or a partnership to the person you feel can help you. However, if the fear of moving forward, with certain aspects of your life, is crippling to you, then perhaps there are deep wounds inside your energy field, possibly from childhood traumas. These fears cripple your every move toward something fruitful, whether it is getting a degree, starting a business, or even getting the girl or the guy. These fears block you from the awareness that these things exist within your realm of possibility. These are your unconscious fears stored in the subconscious mind. Because the conscious mind cannot see into the subconscious mind, it is difficult to see the fears that exist there. However, you can bring these subconscious fears into the light of your consciousness and be rid of them. How can you get rid of something that you have no knowledge of? Read on.

Fear Breeds Destruction

Some fears are deeply rooted in the recesses of our subconscious mind. These undiscovered fears are caused by various sources. They can be handed down from past generations, or through our parents, or cultivated through our own personal afflictions. There are also unconscious fears caused by physical or psychological abuse or, in some cases, perceived abuse during the early developmental years. These are possibly the most prominent fears we have. They were created by the subconscious mind during our childhood innocence, in an attempt to protect our fragile mental state. However, these fears can solidify into our most hardened blockages, which in turn create irrational habits and tendencies that develop during our teenage years and into our adult life.

If you believe that fear is a necessary element for life, you are right, but what are its obligations? How can we more appropriately view, interpret, and deal with these crucial messages that are brought to us through fear? We can see the devastation of fear when left unnoticed in our own life and in the lives of others. We have felt the dread of fear in our body through shifts in our emotional and mental states. The effects of fears can be debilitating and can morph into severe afflictions in the physical, mental, emotional, and spiritual bodies. Fear can paralyze us from making forward movements. It can impact our rationality and our ability to comprehend. It can incapacitate our brain's function and put our physical body in a state of anguish, agony, or distress. But here is the good news: our unconscious fear can be observed, and remedied.

We will explore our recognition and responses to unconscious fears later in this chapter, but for now, let's examine our unconscious reactions to fear and the destruction and depletion of our state of being when we allow the messenger of mind to derail our life.

Beliefs and Fear

As we live and grow, we associate ourselves with or create beliefs or paradigms. We identify ourselves with our beliefs, which shape how we react or respond in certain situations. Most beliefs are unconsciously built on fear, and all our fears are therefore a reaction to something we believe to be true or something we live by. Some beliefs are handed down through generations or acquired during our early developmental years. It makes no difference where they came from or how long they have existed inside our psyche. They control our reactions and habits without our knowing or consent to do so. If we believe something to be true, energy is formed, which supports the mechanics of that belief. And when circumstances bring us face-to-face with that belief, our automatic response takes control.

Similar to thoughts, beliefs are living balls of energy that take homage in the physicality of our body. They exist there, waiting for an opportunity to take control in those moments of our unconsciousness. Unfortunately, for most people, this happens throughout their entire lives. Any extreme fear or emotional reaction we have about something has a direct correlation with a belief we carry about that thing. Since we are here to experience all of life, circumstances will trigger the inner mechanics of those fears or beliefs to allow us to experience the effects of it emotionally. The intent is that we become aware of the existence of that belief or fear and move to release it. For example, boy likes girl; boy moves toward girl and realizes he has a devastating emotional tug inside himself that says, "I am not good enough." Upon investigation, he realizes that he has felt unworthy all of his adolescent life. Now the investigation of how he came to have this feeling becomes his focus. With help, he identifies a wound from his early childhood when he was told by his Mom or Dad that he was not good enough. He understands that through his mental acceptance of this statement, this lie now lives inside his energy field and is blocking him from feeling courageous. Now he moves to release it permanently.

When we become aware of our fears, the possibility presents itself for us to become aware of the mental definition that created the belief or fear. For example, fear of expanding or going beyond where we currently are is fear of the unknown. The mind tells us that in order to move forward, we must know what is waiting ahead. If we know, then we can control the situation. And if we don't know, then we will not be in control. Control is the measurement we use to manipulate the result of our actions or non-actions. When we don't like the unknown, simply because it is unfamiliar, we feel that we can neither understand it nor control it beforehand. These types of fears may have developed in our childhood years from our being afraid of the dark, or of something we could not see. In our adult life, our fear of moving forward may be related to a definition that says, "I can only move forward if I am certain of the outcome." Our psyche lets us know, through a severe emotional tug when we try to move forward that we have these limiting beliefs. The fear becomes so great that it forces us to awaken to the fact that we have unconscious beliefs. Once identified, once the fear has been brought into the light, we can transform the fear into lightness. The fear will dissipate, and we are never haunted by that particular fear again. Both conscious and unconscious fears can be observed and remedied, but the process requires patience, practice, and investigative work.

Humans and their indulgence in fear have caused fear to proliferate into a destructive force on this planet. But we can change that. Fear exists to tell us that we have a belief that is out of alignment with who and what we truly are. Fear is like a flat key on the piano that must be retuned: change the definition of the fear and bring it back into harmony with who we are. Have the knowledge that fears are there to serve us. Then we can transform fears into inspiration. The size of the fear typically parallels the size of the core issue within our psyche that has been distorted by that fear. And the size of the core issue is parallel to the height of our transformation once the fear has been recognized and released. The awareness of any overwhelming negative energy in us brings an opening for us to transform the energy, to propel us toward freedom from fears.

In the stillness of mind, emits the light of consciousness.

Anticipation of Change

The very quality of a fear, the nature and structure of a fear can be observed. Once observed, the understanding of that particular fear can be examined and then applied to other neurotic fears, such as fear of time, fear of the past, and fear of the future. But this process must be done perfectly. It must be done in the absolute presence of a still mind, with utmost care, so as not to reproduce or reengage any old fear or to create new ones. Once recognized consciously, the fear will dissipate and have no further hold on us. It is gone—finished. The reckless and elusive habits attached to that fear will disappear. We will consciously notice ourselves with new habits, which will surprise us at first and we will be pleased. We will feel lighter, at ease, and less afraid to meet and conquer other rogue fears.

What would happen in our life if we could feel and see our fears, thank them for the knowledge they bring, and move on? What or who would we become without fear? We cannot truly know life or enjoy life while being possessed by fear. The absence of fear would bring tremendous freedom from within. Now we want to investigate the hidden fears to look at and expose them, bringing them into the light. But how do we do this, since the fears were created by us through mind? Looking at fear and getting rid of fear is neither a theory nor a hope. It is a journey onto itself. It requires that we become consciously aware. To begin the journey, do not bog the mind with aimless wondering as to whether or not it can be done. Free yourself from idle conclusions. When the mind is still and free from idle thought, abundant energy flows. In this state of mind, fears are easily observed and recognized when they arise. Become present.

Be Present

Before you attempt to apply this ritual, you must practice. You must become the observer, without engaging the thinker (thought). You can become present by embracing what the five senses are revealing to you, but without engaging thought. The mind sees, but the thinker is not engaged. This means, as you go about your day, you need only to look, observe, feel, and embrace, without thought, judgment, or presupposition, and without labeling. Learn to observe everything, but without engaging thought. This creates a still mind, and from that space of stillness, you become the observer, without the thinker. Certain breathing exercises and certain yoga postures (discussed in later chapters) will also assist in harmonizing the conflict between body and mind and will relax you deeper into a state of stillness, even as you move about.

Exercise 1

Go to the park, by the water, in a wooded area, or on a busy street—anywhere that is comfortable for you—and just watch and feel. Watch the birds moving about, without engaging thought. Hear the waves crashing upon the shore, but just listen. Watch people as they move about in their busy day, without thought. Watch and listen to little children, without thought. Stop for a drink and feel the cold or warmth of the liquid as it meanders down your throat. Pay attention to the taste of it, without thought. Watch and listen to the seagulls; listen to conversations and observe people's reacting to each other. Listen to your footsteps as you move down the avenue; feel the gentle breeze caressing your skin; see, feel, hear, taste, and smell, and do all of this without engaging thought. Do this until you have developed the discipline to become the observer. This creates space, internally and externally. Space is necessary for the journey on which you are about to embark—the journey of ridding fear, the journey to self-discovery.

Exercise 2

Sit or lie in a posture for meditation. Take a few breaths to still the mind. When you become aware that you have entered that space of stillness, mentally ask your fears to reveal themselves to you, and wait. Do not ask for any particular fear, for your subconscious mind is your higher mind and is the holder of your unconscious fears. It knows what to reveal to you and will become the gatekeeper for bringing fears to the surface in their own time. Just be still, be patient, and wait.

When a fear comes up, just notice it. Observe it in the stillness of mind. Do not engage thought or worry or become afraid. Just look at it. If feelings of discomfort produced by the fear arise, just be with them. Allow the discomfort to move through you unencumbered. Watch the physicality in the body and see where the discomfort resonates and how it feels. Experience the feelings of the fear in the present moment, with your full awareness. Be grateful for what you are experiencing, for this is the beginning of your evolutionary process away from a mind-indulgent life. This is the beginning of a new day, with new experiences and the path to a benevolent life. Pay full attention to what you are feeling, since for the first time, and with your full awareness, you are experiencing the physicality of fear, knowing in this moment that without the light of your consciousness, these dark energies would be wreaking havoc inside your body, creating blockages and a myriad of other predicaments. Now your awareness is simply watching the effects of the fears in your body. Your mind is still and watching without provocation. Your ability to watch and feel the movement of the fear without becoming engaged causes the fear to run its course, void of any damage to your body, *and it is done*. The fear dissipates. It is gone and you feel lighter.

Trust yourself and your body's ability to reveal the many fears and obstructions as you continue to do these exercises daily. Fears will be revealed to you in their own systematic patterns and in their own time, but always when you are in the stillness of mind. Remember you are not in control, so just be with whatever comes up. If you remain steadfast, tremendous shifts will take place in the level of your awareness. You will begin to see your life unfolding before you. You will begin to understand the subtleties of the movement of the life you lead through your emotional content. You will come to realize the true meaning of being consciously aware. As your awareness increases, you will have flashes of truths, the orchestrations of life being revealed to you in small doses, with deep understandings, which is wisdom. You will understand that everything has a purpose and its own time. This brings about a feeling of absolute and utter peace. And your life becomes simple. Your awareness is growing.

The human body and the mind are intelligent and sophisticated instruments. They will bring up fears in perfect timing. Typically, the fears that relate to core issues inside your energy field—the ones needing to be resolved in the now—are brought up in their own systematic form. The resolution of these fears will cause momentous shifts in your psyche. Your awareness will grow and your habits will change, and you will feel yourself becoming lighter. Your evolutionary process has begun. Continue to do the exercise of ridding fears daily. The more you do it, the less cluttered you become and the closer you move to getting in touch with the self. Fear fragments and blocks your energy, numbing its effect in your body. When fears have been removed, fresh energy is established and produces a radical inward transformation. Stay alert and be with the shifts as they occur inside your being. They bring about feelings of freedom and revitalization. You act from a place of balance, lightness, and peace. A mind that has no fear is limitless and capable of many great things.

As life is, so are we. We are alive, always moving and flowing, never resting. Freedom requires that everything of the past remains in the past, so that the mind is always fresh, innocent, and full of vigor. It is only in this state that one can truly observe, and the observing is learning. To observe requires your full awareness of what is going on inside you, without attempting to make any modifications. This is a journey of discovery into the most secret crevices of the subconscious mind. Travel lightly by releasing burdens, opinions, prejudices, and conclusions. Rekindle your innocence and see yourself for the first time.

Journaling for self-healing, also called "automatic writing," is another forum for self-discovery of insights into what is going on inside you. It is not just about keeping track of your progress and growth. The act of journaling activates spirit, your higher self, to speak to you through what comes out on paper. Journaling is the flow of intuition in writing. I have practiced journaling many times and found that, at some points, my thoughts stop, and the flow from the divine continued through me, through the pen, and on to the pages. This is divine light flowing through you. When you read what you have just written, you will know that you have been guided and that what was written is wisdom, pure and simple. The wisdom you received is not just on the pages of your notebook, but is also in you. It is a good practice to journal often to get in touch with your higher self. Ask questions of your higher self and journal the answers. Through journaling, you will realize that the distance between you, the awareness, and the divine is no space. Journaling is meditation in writing.

The Far Recesses of Mind

Let's examine a not-so-obvious solution to another aspect of fear that may come about through unproductiveness, stalling, fear of moving forward, or fear of not knowing how to proceed. I will demonstrate using one example of my own relationship with mind.

I mentioned under "My Youth Sprung forth Wisdom" that I recognized early on that I had abilities with mind. What is mind? Mind is a tool that is spirit, which can be used to guide us, to bring us information, and/or to relay knowledge. This knowledge can be within the bounds of earth, or it can be outside the bounds of earth, into other worlds or galaxies. While it may feel to most that we all have our own mind, the raw truth is that we live in an ocean of mind and of consciousness. Mind and consciousness are everywhere. Mind has access, therefore, to the entire recesses of this universe. We all have access to information and creativity that exist beyond time and space. We call those who have displayed brilliance in music or art or industry geniuses. We look to the likes of Ludwig van Beethoven, Vincent Van Gogh, and Nikola Tesla and feel that we are less than, relative to their ability to bring newness and freshness onto this planet to improve our lives. We believe them to be far ahead of everyone else because they had the abilities to use mind. But the truth is that we all have access to the full spectrum of mind for all the brilliance it can relay to us. And all that is required is our desire to go beyond what is already known. Mind is spirit; therefore, there is nothing in this universe that is separate from us relative to our abilities to access and understand them. We must adapt the awareness regarding the vast reaches of mind. Most geniuses were simply deep in thought when they recognized that the skies opened up and furnished them with brilliance beyond their wildest imagination. Therefore, one of the criteria for allowing mind to go deeper into the far reaches of the universe is intense concentration. Know that any exceptions one can create on this planet are available to all in the same or similar degree. For even while wearing human skin, we are spirit and have access to tools that are of spirit. Thusly, nothing is outside our reach. We simply need to become aware of this truth.

While designing and building luxury homes in Toronto, I was quite aware that I wanted to include aspects of design and finishing that were unique to each home. I wanted to create what I termed "the dragonfly effect" in each home, which is an air of serenity that can be felt as one enters the home, and could include the kitchen, the bathrooms, and sometimes even the basement. I have always known I possess creativity. But I wanted to go beyond my own creative instincts. What I would do is enter the old home before it was knocked down. I would stand in a particular spot, and in the solitude of mind, with eyes closed, I would begin to imagine how the entranceway should be designed to create uniqueness and flare, in order to bring feelings of serenity to anyone entering the home. I would follow my own thoughts until the revelations stopped. At that juncture, I would simply hold that image in mind and request of mind to take me deeper into creativity, to bring me insights into unchartered creativity that are currently unknown to me. This could take seconds or minutes, but at some point, mind would bring me insights more brilliant than I could have fostered for myself. The trick sometimes was to lay out this epic creative design on paper in full respect of the images I received in mind. This worked for me. It can work for everyone. And the more you can use mind in this fashion, the more brilliant work you can create, and the deeper your understandings of what we are capable of when we use mind properly.

Whatever plans you have, use mind in the same capacity to reveal to you all the steps you require in unison and all the people who have the skills to assist you in one fashion or another. Mind brings brilliance that is universal. Make full use of it.

Ridding Conflicts

Through Patient Practice, You Enter the Temple of Knowledge

One very ordinary morning at approximately 6 a.m., I was awoken with a sudden thud. It felt as if a small thunderbolt had fallen into my stomach and then trickled through my blood and veins until it was everywhere. I hurled myself out of the dregs of sleep and sat up in bed, leaning against the headboard, my eyes still closed, struck in wonder but not frightened. This was my first conversation with God, the first time God spoke directly to me. The feeling in the room was exactly like that of a father addressing his child. The voice was powerful, stern, and hypnotic—the kind to which you want to listen and absorb everything being said, but without any retort. I sat there like a baby in a crib. "Who do you think you are?" the voice said. It was not a question. It was a command. So let me brief you on some happenings in my life that led to this thrashing from the Almighty.

As far back as I can remember, I thought my mother was quite beautiful. I thought she was rather classy and elegant, sophisticated and very much a lady. She had stature. Those may not have been the exact words that came to mind then, but by the age of sixteen, the essence that personifies those qualities was the biggest attractor for my interest in young women. There were many such females over the years and I adored them all. I was aware of the power and allure of the feminine essence and form and was captivated by it. So up to the age of twenty-four, I indulged in many alliances with women, loving them in the moments but without commitment—never taking into consideration their hearts. There were broken hearts and many tears. I had developed a rationale for my behavior, which was that when something is plentiful or given freely, one holds no reverence for it. My awareness knew that this was wrong, and I felt some guilt, but the sweetness of the female would override that guilt every time so I continued. But something else was bogging my mind. I wondered why these young women, who were so beautiful, sensual, and appealing, would give themselves to me so easily. So here was the paradox: on one hand, I was enjoying the sweetness of the feminine, and on the other, I was judging them for their lack of self-respect. That troubled me for some time. The mind, when left unchecked, can wander off on its own, creating conclusions that we unconsciously hold on to as our own. Where was my empathy for hurting others? Let me answer that: it was a faint abstraction in my awareness at the time, because the physical clearly outweighed the spiritual in the absence of a higher mind.

And so the Almighty spoke to me.

> Do you not know that the feminine has tremendous influence in this world in which you live? Don't you know that the feminine are the givers of life, the nurturers of a unified whole, the integrators of completeness and harmony, whose roots are deep in their hearts? Do you not know that they are the holders of a powerful intuitive force? It is the feminine that possess the energy of the goddess that polarizes the masculine to bring about balance and transformations on the planet. It is the feminine that encourage a state of "being," which itself brings stability.

God's thrashing went on and on for what may have been ten minutes. When it was over, I noticed that the front of my shirt was lathered in tears and the beating of my heart was heavy and loud. I sat immobilized for some time before I could move, but in that time, many things happened. I was forever changed. My beating heart had garnered deep compassion and care to function lovingly from this time and moving forward. I felt a deep shame for my attitude toward the feminine and a deep sympathy for the hearts I had broken, and the tears I had caused to flow. I felt momentous guilt for the lies I had told. I felt dishonorable for the judgments I had cast upon the female. I realized for the first time that those beautiful young women were someone's children, and without thought, I reached for my phonebook and began the process to rectify my bad judgments. I called as many of the women as I could reach, and from deep within, I bathed them with apologies and begged for their forgiveness. They cried and I cried. I told them that I recognized the pain I had caused and that I would not repeat this behavior with others. They cried some more. They told me that they thought I was different, unique, and that they had really hoped we could've been together; we cried some more.

Later that evening, I called others and went through the same ritual as before, and when it was done, I felt wholly cleansed from inside—mind, body, heart, and intellect. The result of that interaction with spirit brought forth a new mind in me, a new look and feel of who I was to become, in a new skin. Thereafter, women have a much deeper influence in my life, beyond intimacy. I see them differently, as they are, in their glory. With a new mind, what I feel for the feminine is beyond respect. It is beyond honor. I feel a reverence for them all. They are the goddesses that can cause men to become honorable, true, and just. It is their innate power of goodness, fairness, and equanimity that has kept life on this planet in some form of balance. Every female I look upon, I see and feel her prowess and grace. Irrespective of their physicality, I now see or sense their uniqueness, and their uniqueness is their beauty that cannot be denied or altered by anyone. I have since developed many female friendships, which are broad and true and void of ego. True power comes through their natural intuitive grasp, for they are truly mothers of the earth.

Notice how the mind can drag you easily into becoming your own worst nightmare, creating conflicts and leaving rubble of sadness in its wake, both for you and for others. When people are not in awareness, they are easily led by simple mind. And simple mind knows neither truth nor compassion. It knows only how to blame, criticize, and complain. It is simple mind that has no care for others and judges easily. It is simple mind that has you think only of yourself. It is simple mind that creates your beliefs and paradigms, which later create a battlefield for you against life. It is simple mind that creates fears of advancing your life. The job of simple mind is to keep you simple, for within its confines is a lack of productive and harmonious energies. The readings below reveal how to remove the conflicts and debris that bog the mind and haunt your life. It prepares you to move to a higher, more productive mind. And all that is required is stillness.

Something else has happened to me through this experience. I have become a "balanced man." I knew of the masculine and feminine energies but was unsure of their broader meaning. After being told by several women that I was the only balanced man they know, I sought to find out exactly what I had been led into through divine orchestration or through my own semi-unconscious accord. Interestingly, in my thirties, I was very inquisitive and loved to take something interesting and explore it to near infinity. I had gone on a quest for information on loves that had stood the test of time. I spoke to many couples that had been together for long periods, between thirty and fifty years. I was interested in what caused their relationships to last. The original answers were not what I expected. I expected it to be about lasting love and how to nurture that love. But from the men, it was more about learning when to "shut up" and not bother to argue with their wives, else the battle would go on and on.

I saw clearly through these explorations that men and women did not truly understand each other's internal properties. My own intuition had become stronger over time. Thusly, during conversations with men and women, I could intuit a lot more about them than the words they were relaying. I sensed that men and women saw things differently—the world, life, and living—and responded to these things differently. From looking deeper, I saw that men were far more in their heads or minds, more interested in exploring things and always wanting to move to or to create the next best thing or place, striving, organizing, wanting to structure, and the like. I noticed that women were more nurturing, more sensitive, more receptive to things and situations, living and speaking from the heart, and I recognized that their intuitive senses are a force. I sought even deeper and became aware of the energies on earth that were the masculine and feminine and their relations in harmonizing life and balance on the planet. Yin and yang create universal balance, and this is necessary, for where there is no balance, chaos becomes functionally present. Planet earth requires the balance of the masculine and feminine energies, which together create a natural perfection. The feminine energy governs nature; the masculine energy governs spirit. This forms the collaboration of natural synchronicity in its grandest form. But our recent history has thrown this balance off course since it has been forged by the masculine perspective alone, being directed toward goals defined by the masculine alone, and this includes the goal to control. There is now a deep impulse on earth to balance these two energies within ourselves and throughout the entire human culture. And we must accomplish this.

So what is a balanced man? I remain quite masculine, but I have become more approachable by the feminine. I understand them and feel them deeply, and they sense my neutrality and my supportiveness of the feminine. They are aware of my reverence for them and my having a natural understanding of them. They sense that I can feel their emotions, and they can feel mine. Having more female friends has caused my intuition to grown significantly. I can sense when a conversation should be steered off the present course; I feel my own emotions more broadly than before; anything that touches my heart deeply sometimes does cause tears to come to my eyes; I am a defender of any unjust acts I see. I am even more sympathetic to animals and bugs in that I cannot kill a spider or a bothersome fly. I am receptive to what others have to say; I have recognized the ability to rest in a state of surrender, allowing life to flow to me and through me. Thusly, I see things more clearly, I argue far less than I used to, I have become very open to listening broadly, and understanding others well, and my relations with the female are comfortable and supportive. Many of my female friends ask for my advice about the men they meet during their dating processes. They trust my instincts. I have arrived at valuing all women as I value my own mother and my daughter.

A Fragmented Self

You are being prepared to embark on a journey of self-discovery where the object to be discovered is the "self." Who is the self? It is not your body and it is not your mind, and it is not your personality. It is the essence and flavoring of the divine, a spark of radiant light with infinite possibilities that live inside you, and *is you.* But how do you find the self, when you have systematically and unconsciously buried it under layers of debris created by simple mind? Through your likes, your dislikes, your non-acceptances, and your judgments of others and things, you have become lost. Through your irrational patterns of thinking, your reactions to what you consider good and not good, and your created characteristics, paradigms and beliefs, you have become even further lost. So who is it that is judging and disliking? And who is observing?

There is only one life. This will be so today, tomorrow, and for evermore. Everything that lives, breathes, moves, grows, shifts, etc., is a part of that one life. All of humanity is bound together and shares in this one life with the birds, bees, oceans, mountains, and trees—everything. So when you look at someone or something and observe what you like or dislike about that person or thing, you have created a separation between you and that person or thing. This separateness begets chaos in your being (the self) and in your life. Through the unconsciousness of your irrational (simple) mind, you are fragmenting yourself, which is the self you seek. If you take a rock and with hammer and chisel, continuously chip away at the rock, at some point there is no rock. What is left is only rubble; so is the case with you. Every time you judge or point the finger or blame, or push others or things away from you, you are chipping away at and diminishing your self. In your fragmented state of being, the task of knowing the self, who you truly are, becomes a daunting task, like trying to find a black hole in the dark. You continue to feel lost and confused, yet you continue to create more separateness and mental turmoil inside and outside yourself. You are constantly judging, which further separates you from the oneness with life that we all seek. If you come to recognize your chaotic state and want to clear the rampant and fruitless patterns from your mind, you realize that you don't know how. Simple mind left to its own device is reckless, and the effect of its recklessness drags you into deep waters, where you become further fragmented, unhealthy, and lost.

How then do you identify your self in all these mental abstracts you have formed? The human psyche is made up of memories: past experiences, good and bad happenings, ethnic or cultural pressures/traditions, and your own distress. All of this has formed your character. Take time to notice that it is all the past. So you, the observer, are a culmination of both your past and your present. If tomorrow is unpredictable, you will shift again to accommodate whatever colours your perception and attitude. And since your consciousness is not present in all of this, the only thing that exists in you is turmoil. While in this state of disorder, you have no solid reference point from which to see or solve the problem within or without yourself. Your orientations are solely in the past and were never fruitful to begin with. Where in all of this is the observer, the one looking at this chaos?

At any given point, one can either be in the realm of ego mind or in the realm of consciousness. When you continue to create judgments on things you perceive as outside yourself, you are separating yourself from consciousness while remaining steadfastly stuck in ego mind. Ego mind is not the way to the self. In fact, ego mind restricts you from finding who you truly are. Ego mind provides you with false perceptions and illusions, so you continue to create and recreate yourself in absolute falsity. This keeps you in a state of not really knowing who you are at any point in time. Now you are maddened with conflicts, wondering who you are and how to easily identify yourself. You want to separate yourself from all the baggage you have created through ego mind, to arrive at a point of certainty about who you are. But you cannot get there from where you are because who you are, "the self," does not reside within the confines of the ego mind.

Let's pause for a moment and take a look at the makeup of mind, since what I have said thus far is that simple mind or ego mind is unproductive and temperamental. There is only one mind, and like awareness, mind has levels, degrees through which one can evolve on the spiritual journey. One aspect of mind can keep you trapped in an illusionary world, never knowing truth. Another aspect of mind develops and holds your greatest desires and brings to you creativity beyond your deepest imagination.

To use mind productively requires stillness. The surface of the mind is always moving, rippling, never still, and never quiet. This surface level is termed the "simple mind." The simple mind is where the ego lives and reigns. Its power is hypnotic and can hold you within its grasp indefinitely when you are not in a conscious state of being. The ego mind is noisy and chaotic and is an entity unto itself. In this state of mind, you cannot inquire into things. You cannot use simple mind to facilitate, properly assess, or assimilate information or choose good from bad. Below is a representation of the degrees of mind. This is my own reference due to the experiences I have had and still continue to have with mind. Perhaps it can be used to guide your understanding of the increases in productivity and power of mind, as you move deeper into mind.

Degrees of Mind

Surface: choppy, erratic, restless, chaotic, burdensome, ego driven.
You are in chaos, living in an illusion, void of substance.

Below the surface: quiet, reflective, contemplative, assessing, organizing.
You feel space, quiet, and silence like being at the ocean and just hearing the sound of the waves as they crest. From the inside, you feel spacious, open, and calm.

Deeper: deep silence, meditative; feel the essence of the spirit.
You feel emptiness, weightlessness, and alive but without form. You realize this is who you are: pure spirit without a body, infinite, and connected to all others in oneness. You are endowed in pure peace, knowingness, awareness and bliss.

Full depth: everlasting stillness—a oneness that is universal.
You feel a connection with the creator, and know that you are one with all there is.

To use the productive energies of the mind, mind must become quiet and still. The stillness brings abundant energies and the far reaches of mind become absolute. How then do you escape the surface mind and sink deeper into the silent space of mind? You do it through the breath. Simply close your eyes and follow the breath. After a few breaths, you will feel the space of calm, quiet, and silence. Know that simple mind (ego mind) can be evolved. It can become fruitful and begin to serve you productively. I will comment more about this in Chapter 3 in the section titled "Lighten Your Load."

Trying to Control

Trying to control creates more conflicts and disorder. Any attempt to control is itself an illusion. You cannot control anything. You cannot control others, and you most certainly cannot control what may happen in the next moment. You cannot control life, because life is as unpredictable as the direction the wind blows in the next moment. Any attempt to control is recognition that you are feeling out of sorts with yourself, creating more separation from the self. But life offers you choices, and when life brings you to a crossroad where there are options, you choose. The choices you make in life are your responsibility.

Beliefs, Paradigms, and Our Guidance System

Beliefs come from many sources: from past lives, from your acceptance or rejection of what your parents believed, from friends, from your culture, and from your unconscious propensity to gain social acceptance. But irrespective of where they came from, the dramas of your life and your ingrained reactions or temperaments are the result of these integrated beliefs. Your life is in conflict because you want something, and life keeps landing you on the opposite side of what you want, and you don't know how to change your circumstances. Life feels like a struggle, but you are unaware of what you are struggling against.

Beliefs are your subconscious mapping of what you have accepted as truth or what you have accepted as useful to regulate your life. Your subconscious mind is your director. It directs your movement with life in accordance with the things you have accepted as truths. The things you have accepted as truths are energy. They are real, and they live inside your system of energy. All your beliefs will bring into the forefront experiences or feelings that will allow you to see and feel the ramifications of your belief in daunting fashion, such that you notice what you are creating. You wonder why your life is the way it is—why you cannot establish certain things in your life, whether it is money, good health, happiness, or lasting love. But how can you find out what these deep-rooted beliefs are, since they are unconscious? Once they are known, can anything be done about them?

As you will explore later in this book, your human body is far more sophisticated and complex than you can imagine. The human body resides at the junction where spirit meets matter. You are a culmination of spirit and matter working cohesively together.

Cosmic energy flows down through the crown chakra and into the energy system throughout your spinal column called chakras. The purpose of the chakras is to accept and regulate the cosmic energy flow, which causes your body to function at its optimum capacity, and pass to you knowledge, through the emotions you feel, of what you have accepted as truths. The emotions you feel are therefore the outcome of your thoughts, your beliefs, and the paradigms you have accepted and hold dear, whether they are extreme negativity, fear, love, or passion. Pay attention to your emotions, for they shine a light on your unconscious patterns of thoughts and beliefs.

Chakras also communicate with you in regard to decisions you are about to make, through feelings. You feel through your emotions. And through your emotions, your energy systems guide you with decisions, using feelings of heightened vibrations, such as feelings of love, simply "feeling good," or adversely, through feelings of lower vibrations like fear, uncertainty or "not feeling good." This is your universal internal decision-making guidance system at work. Pay attention. At the recognition of every decision you are about to make, become still for a moment and feel from the inside. What is your internal guidance system (your emotions) telling you? Become ardently aware.

Living centered on meditation requires no control. The continuous awareness harnesses and sharpens your intelligence. You see your contradictions and ambiguities as they arise. You are fastidiously learning, for the seeing and understanding is the awareness, and you are being transformed. Meditation relieves you of the desire to control, and in this way, there is no conflict. Meditation also relieves you of the propensity to hold on to beliefs, since they restrict your flow with life. Instead, meditation furnishes you with the wisdom to seek truth, your truth from within, which brings about a deeper awareness—a decree of knowing.

Watch the desires that arise in you. You don't need to do anything about them. You don't need to yield to them or to suppress them. Just watch them as you would watch daylight fall to dusk. Be fully aware of what is happening: the coming of the desires and the falling off of the desires. Watch the beginnings and the endings of thoughts, as you would notice that the end of sleep is the beginning of awake. Just watch. Then there is no control and no disorder.

Understanding Meditation

Pranayama is life energy generated by controlled breathing. Make it the beginning of your meditation. It brings vitality, quiet, and calm. Be patient with the breath. Allow it to become synchronous on its own, with its own rhythm. Relax into the breath, for it is your doorway to consciousness. Your wanting to meditate is your calling to know who you are, to remember who you are. Meditation will take you to a depth of stillness and sanctity, allowing you to sense and feel who you are. And when you do, you will desire to be in constant touch with your eternal self, for herein is a place of absolute stillness, grace, love, calm, and power. The feeling of divinity will pervade you. It is a feeling beyond words, for in and through it, you feel your true "being" and you will know who you truly are. Your wanting to reconnect with who you truly are is now sanctified, for you are on a one-way journey home to the self.

Meditation transforms you into knowing who you are, and it brings with it courage and a desire for you to never stop reaching. Through your deep longing to reconnect, meditation brings you to your center. Your life experiences become an entranceway for your remembrance. Pay attention to your feelings and emotions. They are not accidents. They are guides to be used to access the fullness of your very being. They are your access from where you stand into the fullness of your being, which is who you are. Be aware of the subtleties of emotions. Realize their value to you and to leading you to your center. This is your only job on earth, to return to the self, and know who you are. This vantage point will begin to lift you out of the illusion on this planet. You will begin to see everything in your life—the ups and the downs and the sideways—as infinitely beautiful. When so-called problems arise, don't be tormented by the pain. Realize that pain takes you into the deepest recesses of your being, from which, if you are consciously aware, new things will be revealed to you about your life. Pain is an avenue for looking deeper inside, and when you look, the missing links will reveal themselves.

Meditation gives you access to infinite energy. When you are embedded in consciousness, you will feel infinite love, more deep and sacred than anything you have ever imagined, so deep that time stands still; minutes will seem like hours. Now you are aware of the depth and essence of which you are a part, and of the tremendous love and compassion innate in your being that is beyond words. You feel the absolute bliss of your existence and know that you are eternal.

Meditation, a Transformative Tool

Meditation should cover all aspects of your life, for it is not separate from any part of your life. It should cover your job, your business, your relationships, the things that trouble you, the things that bog the mind, etc. It should cover your pleasures, your likes and dislikes, your desires, and your struggles and triumphs. It must cover everything, or it is pointless as a transformative tool.

Becoming awake is watching everything that happens—the good, bad, and the puzzling. This watching or looking must happen in the present moment. This does not mean you sit around and do nothing. The mechanics of who you are is far more sophisticated than one can imagine. Go about your daily business as usual, but keep your mind alert, open, and not intoxicated with the constant nonsense that has been regulating your life thus far. Do what you need to do, but from the space of stillness. From that space, you become the doer, the analyzer, and the observer in every moment. For example, you may feel emotions arise when dealing with someone and realize that you carry resentments toward them. But now you are the watcher, so simply watch. Watch the feelings inside your body; sense where they are in your body and feel the physicality or discomfort. Just watch and feel, but do not engage thought or try to modify what you are feeling. The awareness has now been revealed to you in the present moment. You have become aware of something that lives inside you, something that was hidden from your consciousness. Now you can do something to release it from your body. You have become the watcher of your own self and your life as it unfolds from within. Your awareness will deepen and your life will become more fruitful. This is meditation. Live it in your waking hours every day.

If your mind is occupied with the past, and that preoccupation converges with the present, then you are unconscious, lost, and asleep. Meditation, as a tool, is the nexus for seeing what's taking place in all facets of your life, including all the contradictions, challenges, denials, and conflicts that possess your being every day—all the days of your unconscious life. Meditation is therefore not something you do just at night or in the early morning. It is continuous. To do it properly, you must live in that state every waking moment, always watching and looking for what comes to the forefront, for it is all about you. It can never be about someone else. You need to cultivate that space, that stillness, that void, so deep and probing that you sense its enormity. At any given moment, simply become still and focus on the breath. This will create a space, and space is vital and necessary for the revelation of the pieces of conflict and unrest that operate inside your being. Meditation, therefore, is not separate from daily living. It converges with it.

Realize then, that you are responsible for yourself, and therefore, for the part you play in the totality of life on this planet. Do not allow this truth be a weight on your shoulder. Simply play your part with your best intentions by being the best "you" that you can be. Become responsible for yourself and for your relationship with others. Plant the seed in mind that you affect the entire world with who you are and what you put out into the world. Face the fact that what you think, what you feel, and how you act has an effect on the world in which you live. Do not become strained. This knowledge should not be daunting to you. Simply realize that you play a part, and play that part from the core of your being. Getting to and aligning with your true self should become your courageous journey. For when you know and love yourself, and feel love and kindness toward others, you will cease pointing fingers and casting blame.

If you can do this, if you can take responsibility for yourself, if you can do this irrespective of what others around you are doing, if you can remain in the true essence of your being, then you will be bringing about a psychological transformation in the minds and hearts of man on our planet. This transformation will ease the pain of violence, hate, separation, anxiety, fear, greed, envy, brutality, wickedness, and all of the idiocy that man has perpetuated on this planet thus far.

To do this, observe yourself in your daily life. See what's taking place inwardly and outwardly. Do not rely solely on your already acquired knowledge, for that has been tainted, fragmented, misaligned, and thwarted. Your journey and knowledge must now involve the totality of life on this planet—everyone, not just yourself. To do this, you simply look at the process of life within you. This process of life shows you that the inner conditions of your life are always harmoniously related to your outer circumstances, which you have consciously or unconsciously created through your mental attitude. What you think, believe, or accept from inside yourself, you create. That creation expresses itself as the circumstances you encounter in your outer life. When your outer circumstances are harmonious with your inner creation, everything is good. However, most of the time, you do not like the circumstances of your outer life but are unaware that you created them from your internal process of life. This is the movement of life to which you must pay attention to create balance and harmony within yourself, to ensure that your inner creation and your outer conditions are harmoniously in sync.

At first you were unconscious of the relationship between your inner and outer life, and now you are aware of it. You simply watch this movement and come to understand what is happening inside and outside of you. This is learning and knowing yourself, for the recognition of the inner and outer movements is the awareness, and where there is awareness, there is knowledge and growth. The result is that your transformation takes form. This is the only thing you need to conquer. And if you can do this earnestly, you will resolve your own conflicts and be transformed. This will bring about a psychological shift in all of humanity not unlike hitting the reset button.

Creating a Fertile Mind

Who we are affects life and we are then affected by the life we co-create. Can man cultivate a new virtue, a fresh mind to create a new world, a new beginning? If this is to be, we must become responsible for ourselves, irrespective of our race, culture, or where we were born. We must completely understand that we, humankind, must become completely responsible for the entire state of humankind. We are all responsible for all the injustices that are happening around the globe, fueled by the antagonism of our own lives and by our selfishness, our prejudices, our perceived principles—all of which divide us. Only when we truly understand the intrinsic oneness of humankind will we recognize that you and I are responsible for all this existing chaos and misery. But we, as individuals, must change this. Do not look to anyone else. Look instead inside yourself, and find the courage to express your best self. Embrace life with your best dance. Live by your truest expression of divinity.

Where there is difference, there is conflict, but why should there be any conflict? What you think bears only on you and no one else. Care and attention are required to look at issues or problems that create the relationship between your inner self and your outer knowing. If there is no attention on yourself, then you create conflict by looking at others and judging or labeling, which does not create oneness. We all have our issues; therefore, we are all the same. Treat others as you would treat yourself, without the labels. See them as yourself. Then there is no division and no labeling and, therefore, no conflict. This starts with understanding yourself.

On the opposite side of sacredness is chaos. So what is sacred to you? Start with yourself when looking for anything sacred, but you must first get rid of the chaos, that is your fears, your despair, and the ills of your past pains. When you are free of all of this, you can move on to great things. Sacredness becomes apparent when fear is dissolved—when we see what is happening inside us and when we see what is happening between others and ourselves in relationships or friendships. Sacredness is having insight into what is happening inside you. It is a deep insight of what and who you are right now. It is an immediate observing and knowing of your own consciousness.

We are fragmented so we only see the bits and pieces of ourselves that do not require diligent attention. Attention comes when the mind is silent, uncluttered, unattached, and without movement. This creates a fertile mind where there is no attachment to country of origin, to culture, to prime minister, to wife, or to husband. When you love, attachments become unnecessary. Someone tells you that you are beautiful, and you say thank-you. That's it. There is nothing to hold on to, so there is no attachment. If you require attachment, you will bring back the mental cluttering to torment your life. An attached mind is an unhealthy mind. Conversely, a healthy mind is without conflict. When you understand this at a great depth, it becomes a part of you. Then mind becomes sacred.

Can you do this? Can you take a courageous stance for yourself and for humanity to do this work? Can you look ahead and see a world refined with people who care for and cherish all others? A world where honor and harmony prevail? If you believe you can do this, let's take this journey together.

The Journey Inward

The Door to Immeasurable Sacredness

I n August 1998, I was involved in a near-death automobile accident. I woke up one morning, like any other morning, except something was different. I realized I could not move. I thought that perhaps I was in a dream so I opened my eyes to ensure I was not dreaming. I could see my bedroom and the bathroom, but I was still unable to move. I tried calling out for my fiancée, but words did not come. An ugly irking sound made its way from my jaws, and she came running into the room. "I can't move," I said frantically. "Please, hon lie back. I have something to tell you."

"Okay, but I want to sit up."

"No," she said. "It's better if you stay lying down. Do you remember anything over the past five days?"

I was utterly clueless as to what she was referring to. "No," I said. "I went to bed, and now I am waking up."

She asked me not to move and went into the bathroom, bringing back a mirror. She held the mirror in front of my face, and I did not recognize myself. I had never been so shocked in my life. There was no face, at least not mine. What I saw was something favoring wood that had been run over several times by a very large truck. That was not my face.

The story goes that five days prior, I was involved in a four-car collision. The report from the Paramedics and police stated that my car was first broadsided by a vehicle running through a stop sign and unto a major four-lane highway. My vehicle had been hit so hard that it was pushed across two lanes and into oncoming traffic. I was hit again by two vehicles moving westbound. The two westbound drivers and I were badly hurt, two of us with severe brain injury. My head had crashed through the windshield, rendering me unconscious.

My fiancée advised me that I had been in the hospital for a few days, in and out of consciousness. The diagnosis was severe brain injury, displaced spinal column in three areas, fractured ankle, broken finger, right ear torn off, and over 130 stitches in my face, plus many shards of glass still embedded in my head and forehead. She also advised that I became conscious intermittently in the hospital and pleaded vehemently with the doctors to let me go home.

I have always hated the smell of hospitals, and being in and out of consciousness did not change that. So I asked her why I was not able to move. "Oh," she said, "all the muscles in your body are ripped. They cannot support you right now."

But she was advised that I should try to stand and walk when my body became stronger. As part of the diagnostics, I was advised that some of my brain functions, particularly my executive functioning was skewed; my ability to concentrate was marred; some of my permanent memory had been erased, and my short-term memory would be erratic—there one minute, gone the next.

I spent the next eighteen months undergoing therapy with chiropractors to realign my nearly broken neck and spine, physiotherapy to get my muscles working, functional brain assessment by a neuropsychologist, neurological assessments by a neurologist, and mental assessments by a psychologist. When compiled, it read that I had been knocked back to the cognitive level of a five-year-old. I could not make sense of anything. I did not remember my name, nor did I know what the significance of a name was. I did not know what a country was. I did not know what money was. I did not know how to boil water. I did not know how to relate to others. I developed a rigid angry temperament that was uncontrollable and could be set off by anything, including my own memory losses. I had no memory of the moment before now. I was like a blind fly on a wall with nowhere to go and no knowledge of what to do, how to look after myself, or how to make all this go away. Every time the awareness of my state came to mind, which was often, my eyes would well up with tears.

A few weeks later, my fiancée gave me an envelope she said was for me. I opened it and saw a piece of paper that was green, with numbers written on it. None of it made sense to me, so I ripped it up and threw it in the garbage. The next morning, she woke me up in a frantic manner. She advised me that I had ripped up a check from the major bank for which I was a consultant. The amount was $3,500.00 "What does that mean?" I asked. She advised that it was my paycheck for the week of the accident. "And what is a paycheck?" I asked. She stated it was money. "And what is money?" I asked.

Seven months later, my fiancée had to go back to work. Her place of employment had given her four months to look after me, with reduced pay, but seven months had elapsed, so she had no choice. Once she left the condo, I would sit on the floor with my legs crossed and rock back and forth like a child, not knowing what to do with myself. And on the third day of this senseless rocking, God spoke to me.

The presence of God in the room with me was comforting. I might not have known much of anything else, but I understood the gravity of God's presence, and I felt completely safe. "You are an empty shell," he said. "Now you can rebuild yourself, for your life will be different from this point forth."

I was completely compliant. So I asked, "How do I rebuild myself?" The understanding came that I should educate myself on the person I was, to develop a framework from where to begin the rebuild. The advice was to begin by asking those I trust to describe how they saw me prior to the accident. I followed the instructions and asked four friends whom I knew would be completely direct with me. Interestingly enough, the responses were practically the same. The summary was this: The "me" before the accident was smart, very ambitious and driven, generous with his time in assisting others to go beyond their limits, extremely creative, and quite arrogant at times. Therein, I began the process of rebuilding myself, to empty myself of arrogance and to adapt kindness, gentleness, and empathy. I began by following the waves of intuition as they came.

For the first time in my life, I purposefully meditated, closing my eyes and resting in that place of silence, of stillness. Instructions and answers came. The light of my higher self was revealed to me. I became a listener to the messages and gentle nudges from the spirit realm inside me. As I became aware of the messages from a higher vibration, I arrested myself into the flow of these guiding energies. I resisted nothing, for I knew instinctively that I was being led. I started visiting bookstores, not knowing exactly why I was there, but all the time trusting the knowing from inside me. I became interested in books about meditation and writings from gurus from India and China. I read them many times, and I understood the messages well. I did not know what spirituality was as a name, but I sensed within my being that I was moving toward something quite powerful that lived inside me. I felt that I was being guided by God him/ herself. So I became immersed with the spirit within me.

This was my conscious entry onto the spiritual path. As my awareness grew, realizations came that the automobile accident was no accident, for it had allowed my life to be steered toward my conscious spiritual life. So started the journey of my inner work to "know" my true self. During this time, I read many books and felt grateful in meeting people such as Deepak Copra, Debbie Ford, and Wayne Dyer. I was also lucky enough to spend a short time with Baba Sri Shiva. I have been to a few spiritual meet-ups and have become acquainted with others on the path. In fact, I have formed deep abiding friendships with some. Thus, the journey is not a lonely one anymore.

I remember the day I found Eckhart Tolle's *The Power of Now*. I was wandering around Oakville, near Toronto, with a friend and suddenly found myself being pulled into a store I never would've entered of my own accord. I was alertly aware and followed the vibe. The book drew me to it. I opened it randomly to a page and started to read. Immediately it became infectious. I knew in that instant that this book was what I needed to move to the next level of my evolution. As my evolution progressed, so did the heavenly experiences that came into my seeing, understanding, and knowing. I said in the opening that "heaven exists where we stand." You will recognize that these experiences are beyond the confines of earth and they have given me a solid frame of who I am, and more broadly, who we all are.

The journey inward is a sacred journey. Have you noticed I keep using the word *sacred?* It is for the reason that it's all about you, for the knowing, the truth, and the wisdom come from inside you. You are the awareness, and perhaps for the first time in your life, you will be looking at and learning yourself. For what comes through your awareness is truth. It is real, and it is you. There are neither distortions nor misgivings when you follow the awareness. There is only truth, and you will learn yourself truly and fully. That includes seeing the darkness in you and the lightness in you, and from this sacred space inside you, you will glow with understanding and knowledge of your true self. You will understand that what is in you is also in everyone. Hence, there is no cause for blame or judgment toward anyone, for you are everyone and everyone is you.

Learn Yourself

The journey to the self begins with your awareness that you are not your mind, you are not your body, you are not your personality, and you are not your thoughts, beliefs, and paradigms. None of it. So who or what is the self you seek, and what is your center?

Our most significant false impression is due to the fact that we come to this earthly planet wearing different suits. We come in different colors and shades; we look differently; we think differently; we speak different languages. We therefore fell into the illusion of thought that those people are different from us; they are not us, and therefore we don't trust them – we don't like them. And so on. The deeper we go into this separateness, the farther away we move from knowing and realizing who we truly are. The self is being cloaked behind a mammoth wall of unconsciousness, of blindness, of likes and dislikes, of differences and non-acceptance, and of psychological distancing. When we do this, we are looking through the eyes of simple mind and not through the eyes of consciousness. Simple mind creates fear. Simple mind creates the perception of differences. Simple mind creates separateness. Simple mind casts a dark shadow over our oneness with life. And here is the challenge: to look at all these perceived differences and simply see yourself in everyone. Man created this mask and now we wear it without remembrance of who we are and where we came from. In the midst of all this confusion, how does one find "the self"?

Meditation is the cornerstone for relieving ourselves of the unconscious world we live in. It brings us to our center. Meditation takes us to a place of sacredness and sanctity. Meditation moves us from the illusionary state of perception and furnishes us with awareness, wisdom, and knowledge. It wakens us from our long dark sleep of unconsciousness and lifts us to the clarity of the infinite.

Take a seat for meditation. Breathe. Do not try to control your breath. Simply watch it, allowing it to flow on its own terms. Pay attention to the rhythm of the breath and to the rise and fall of the stomach on each inhalation and exhalation. Just follow the breath, until the breath *seems* to vanish. Now feel. Feel the gentle vibrations inside your body. Feel the space that surrounds you. It is around and through you. You are immersed in it. Recognize the feelings that are percolating through you: feelings of love, joy, peace, and harmony. Feel all that there is. Feel the effortlessness of "being" and the power inherent. Just feel. This is who you are: pure consciousness, pure aliveness, pure power, and pure life. You are soul.

A Single Unitary Force

Contrary to popular assumptions, humankind does not have separate, individual souls. There are not seven billion souls on this planet. There is only one pervasive soul, and we are that soul. We are connected, tied, bound as one unit through time and space. We are one. And in the eyes of everyone we look at, be aware that we are looking at another version of ourselves. We are looking at divinity. No man stands alone or apart from the self. We are one functional unit. When we understand that there is no "them" versus "us," then we begin to understand the prevalent unity that is humankind. Since soul harmonizes as one, no one is here for himself or herself. We are all here for each other, bound together through eternity. There is no singularity in this journey of humankind, no identifiable brain cell that separates one man from another. We are one unit, co-creating life together and co-creating the future together. And in the vastness of this universe of which we are a part, there is no singular unit that functions in and of itself. Realize, therefore, that the unitary self is the culmination of all our neurological mappings to function as one unit and to evolve together as one. It may seem to us that the self we imagine ourselves to be ends at the outer edge of our skin, but we are tied together in mind, soul, biology, and consciousness—all of it. We are one organism. Do not allow the superficial differences, such as birthplace, language, tribe, skin shade, ethnicity, education level, or financial success, be your guide. We are far more complex than the eyes can imagine or the simple mind can conceptualize.

We see each other's physicality and perceive that we are separate, but when we get to know someone, we begin to see the ways in which we are alike. When we look into someone's eyes, if we are looking with a still mind, we will begin to feel a familiarity, a unity with them. That is "divine essence recognizing divine essence." Our emotions allow us, in the now, to experience a feeling of resemblance, an instantaneous knowing that what is in us is also in them, for there is no other. There is only one. We are the universe, a continuous unified ground in a single universal field of existence and intelligence.

Through the whispers from within, my journey with life has proposed many things to me. I became pliable to the nudges and looked forward always to the inherent salvation. I woke up one morning with an impression of wanting to know what oneness was. I held on to that desire. I was curious, but more so, I wanted to feel oneness and become it. There was no direction from the whisper on how I should go about achieving oneness. So I sought it by simply looking at others, including strangers. Simple mind was fanatic in wanting me to know that it is impossible to feel love for others whom I did not know, strangers, who themselves might be crazy or dangerous people. Something inside me wanted to know truth, so I insisted. Whenever I was around others in restaurants, pubs, or outdoor cafes, I would be willfully looking at others. I wanted to see through them, to the inside, to know what lived inside them. I already had the ability to feel inside others when I was in conversation with them. But now I wanted to take that ability to a deeper level—to know how to love completely without even knowing the person. Was this an impossibility? I continued to look at and through others, but nothing came. And after a few dozen attempts, I eased back. I continued to look with full curiosity, but with far less focus.

Some months later, while walking on The Danforth, a place in Toronto that they call Greek Town, I noticed a woman across the street, just as one would notice others for a moment as they pass by. But in this particular moment, something was different. My eyes became transfixed to her and I could not stop looking. As I looked more closely, the realization came from simple mind that I was not attracted to her, yet my eyes were still awestruck in a deep gaze, unable to look elsewhere—enamored—yet my awareness was still unsure of what was happening.

Then suddenly, something magical came forth. I saw and felt her tremendous essence, a movement of radiant energy postulating from inside her and encapsulating her feminine appeal entirely. It was infectious, beguiling, and magnetic, pulling my gaze deeper into this glowing bulb of hypnotic magnetism. I was in awe, my insides vibrating and still steadfastly stuck in the gaze. Then the realization came that I was looking at her soul. Now this female was suddenly ecstatically beaming like a flower in bloom. She was extraordinarily beautiful, intoxicating, and free. My heart raced and I felt pure natural love for her.

This orchestration was an example of mind versus soul. Mind did not find her attractive, because mind is superficial and can only see the physical. But soul is metaphysical and can see the divine light in others. There is nothing more beautiful than seeing the God energy in someone, for the same energy is also in you. This experience was soul recognizing itself. Experiences such as this bring forth understanding and "truth" about who we are. And our awareness will furnish us with the knowledge of the vast differences between looking with simple mind and seeing through the mind of soul.

Sometime later, I started dating a lady named Marilyn. On our second date, we were saying good-bye and again I was struck, held in awe, for her soul was shining through her eyes. I just stood there, unable to move for fear of missing one moment of this wonder. Since that day, whenever I look in her eyes, I see her deeply and feel her God essence somewhere inside my being, as if we are joined. Even when I am not with her, I can feel her energy when it shifts, such as when she becomes sad or when she feels elation.

The realization is that when you see soul in others, there is a merging of the souls. If both people are consciously aware, they will both feel a tremendous shift to a far deeper more abiding love for each other, whether they are friends or lovers. In either case, the relationship will shift to something more sacred, because the merged souls are now bound, forming a unified bond across time and space. The feeling of oneness becomes powerfully present in both parties for all of this life and into other lifetimes. Such relationships will not break, for the two become one. The splendor of being bound to another soul becomes akin to that of identical twins: you feel the person's energy even when they are in another city and you know when they are off their usual vibration. You just feel and you know. You would do everything you could possibly do for this person, if and when they need your help. This is the expression of true love, a love without condition and without limit.

Let me just qualify this by saying when two souls become bound, it does not necessarily mean they must become entangled in a romantic relationship. It could happen also to those who are friends. The ramifications of the friendship or relationship would be the same: their bond becomes deeper, more fruitful, and they come to each other's aid no matter what the circumstances. I have four such female friends, all of whom are highly spiritual. When we get together in the same space, the vibrations percolating in and through us are magnetic, akin to sharing a space with God. Following these experiences, I see beauty and radiance in all others: women, men, children, animals, birds, and the sky. I see others the way soul sees soul—as radiant, glowing beams of infinite light.

There is no personal self. There is only one consciousness, only one universal self that is all of us. We individualize our consciousness through the filter of our nervous system. But the self, the "I" we all refer to, is universal. Now you are aware that whatever you do unto others, you also do unto yourself and unto humanity. Judge no one, for it is a spiritual truth that every trait and characteristic you encounter in others is also present in your own self. That is so, because we are all expressions of the one universal self. We tend to see the defects in other people while turning a blind eye to our own. But sincerity and humility come to us when we realize and accept that every trait that exists in others is also present in us. Seek, therefore, humility in place of arrogance and humble yourself to become totally free from the limitations of ego.

Self-Knowledge

Let's pretend that we are a strand in the unified field that is humanity. Let's further pretend that each strand is responsible for pulling his or her own weight, such that the larger multitudinous force that is humanity can function prosperously and evolve. It is your responsibility to come to know the strand that is you. That is the only unit to which you must develop the fortitude of responsibility. You must come to see and know yourself and understand that you play a part in the whole thing called humanity. Knowing yourself is not a temporary endeavor. It is a journey. The progress you make through self-discovery will increase your awareness and your appreciation for life as it unfolds, both for yourself and for the world. It will give you access to deeper knowledge and wisdom. In this capacity, you will come to understand life on a broader scale and realize that your purpose and the purpose of all of humanity is but one.

Self-awareness is your primary and truest function while you are here on earth. You are the awareness, and the awareness is the observer. But you can only observe when you are consciously aware. Self-reflection brings the unconscious into the light, allowing you to see aspects of your unconscious self that have been blocking you from your own truth, direction, and purpose. Becoming consciously aware brings you to your center, allowing you to see all your misalignments with the life you desire. You take possession of the ability to see clearly what is required to get you where you want to go. Acknowledgment from your center moves you into a state of readiness for change, for spiritual, mental, and psychological growth. Now you know that to become fruitful and walk in your divinity for humanity, you must live from the center, from a place of conscious awareness. Consciousness and its contents are the only reality. Every step of self-awareness is a step toward enlightenment. Meditation is your waking, walking compass: for living, for being awake, for becoming free from the mangle of ego mind, and for allowing the seeds that lie within you to grow and blossom into greatness, to be spread upon the blades of life akin to the magnificent oak.

To become a positively functioning human strand, you cannot be anywhere else but inside consciousness. It is your home, and it is your responsibility. When you are in consciousness, there is no perception and no entanglement with mind, but mind is always with you. When you are consciously aware, mind evolves and your awareness grows, for you are entering a state of grace. Know that your true teacher, your guru, is your inner self. Confide in him or her and be moved toward your goals and your desires. Develop a strong desire to find the self for he or she is present in the heart. Become self-aware, harness self-control, and self-surrender. Exercise earnestness in all you do.

Cultivating Awareness

Who is the witness? It is the awareness. The awareness was always there. It was there at the moment of your conception. It was alive, aware, and present even before you were born onto this earth. Consciousness cannot be observed, for consciousness is spirit, and it is the observer. Your only direct representation of consciousness is through self-awareness. Spirituality is therefore a progressive journey into self-awareness. And when we begin to awaken to the truth of our self, and see and know our self, we feel a hunger to experience higher states of consciousness and blossom into an advanced state of being.

The journey inward is an individual one. No one can help you with it, for your path to the self is just for you. Your journey starts with becoming aware by cultivating a deep sense of present-moment awareness. It is an inner and outer work that requires patience and determination. It is a march you take alone, a march that will reveal great things to you, about yourself, and it will end your suffering and brighten your journey to fulfilling your birthright. Unto he who searches shall it be revealed. The temple of knowledge is available to everyone. Simply knock.

Lighten Your Load

To pave the path for higher consciousness, we must first deal with the baggage we have spent years developing in our unconscious state. We must remold our mind. The mind has very little or no space at all, since we move about with our minds completely occupied with everything at all times. We carry the weight of all our life's stuff; we carry the weight of time, of whatever direction we are heading, or that we are heading nowhere. We carry all replicas of fear, which loves to eat up mind space. We carry our likes and dislikes, our anxieties, negative thought patterns, and the things we fret about. We carry the weight of yesterday, today, and tomorrow. So when is the mind at ease for even a moment? How can man formulate space for himself?

Some people create distractions to stop the chaos. My own distractions were to escape to the theater. I loved the movies and used them as a vehicle for temporary escape from life. Many people use vacations as distractions. Others engage in sports or go for long drives. The distractions usually end and we are back to where we started, for nothing has been achieved. We must learn to cultivate that inner space through meditation and other forms of stilling the mind. When the mind is still, we are immersed in awareness. We are in the place of purity, peace, love, joy, and tremendous stillness. The illusions of life do not exist in this space. When we enter this space, we silently ask "mind" to come with us, for mind evolves along with our awareness. The more space we foster during meditation, the more evolved the mind becomes. The more evolved the mind becomes, the more awareness is bestowed upon us. The more intelligent we become, the more wisdom is imparted to us. Then life becomes blessed, for we are no longer under the illusion that placates this planet. Our intuition becomes sharper, our awareness and spontaneous knowing grows, and we become calm, still, and at peace. Living and being in the flow become sacred.

It is very rare that I open my mouth to answer a question, and the answer comes directly from my mind or intellect. Typically, when I am asked a question, the answers come through me and it is always wisdom that I am hearing and absorbing for the first time. When our awareness grows, we become a vessel. Over the years, I have become accustomed to knowing when my higher self is speaking to me, versus when the messenger is God himself. With my higher self, the answers come in the form of a faint whisper, like a sudden rush of wind that passes over me. His answers typically come to me while I am still asking the question, so I am asking and receiving in the same moment. There have been many occasions when I asked a question and God answered. Answers from God typically fall heavily into my body and percolate to the outer edges of my being like sweet electricity. And the wisdom penetrates up through me and into my awareness. When I am in a gathering or among friends, I don't need to ponder when I should speak. My mouth opens when it is right to do so and the words just come. This is living from awareness, where you are ever present in the here and now. This is being in the flow.

Many things in our lives eat up the mind space, and we don't notice since in the state of a cluttered mind we are sorely unconscious. We must, therefore, purposefully silence the mind, for a still mind brings us to consciousness. Practice self-reflection at night before bed. In this quiet and more relaxed state, simply look over the events of the day. Notice yourself and your patterns and your unconscious habitual cluttering. Notice your likes and dislikes and your reactions to them. And notice the bombardment of all the debris that occupies your mind. This will assist your mind to further evolve. At some point, the mind will take over and become your beacon, even without your inquiry.

My own self-reflections have been broadly revealing. So much so that I actually named some of the methods spirit uses to assist me on the journey of seeing inside myself. The more we self-reflect by looking back over our day, the more spirit will begin to guide us to see ourselves in very uncanny ways, always moving us forward to deeper revelatory insights. And as we grow internally from these insights, our perspective broadens in the moments we are about to step outside our self, for inside those moments, we can change our action or the destination of our words to create more harmony. When I began looking back over my day, higher mind would reveal to me conversations I had had where I made comments that injured or upset the person to whom I was speaking. Through the looking back, the things that were unnoticed by us in the moment of our interactions with others are revealed to us in encouraging fashion. Our entire being becomes engaged in the looking back. Through our hearts and our emotions and all that is love in us, we now clearly see the moments in which we unknowingly caused harm or hurt with our words or our actions.

For example, I would see myself in a conversation with someone and would see and feel how a particular word or phrase I used caused the person some form of emotional unease. I called this one "Woops, too late." This is the spirit in us watching and recognizing this, for the ego mind would never have noticed this. This does not mean that the words I used were wrong in what I was relaying. What it means is that when we are being led by ego mind, we hurt others without knowing it. But when we are being led by spirit, our words and our actions are always refined with love and care, such that there is no harm to others. During self-reflection, we are being guided by spirit; therefore, we become love in its purest form.

As I continued to self-reflect, the revelations became more profound as I recognized the wonders of our internal guidance system. But now, my guidance system is assisting me in the here and now. In this second phase, I am now, in the moment, involved in a conversation with someone. I would be relaying information to someone relative to a task to be completed or one already completed. And this time, I would catch a word or a particular phrase I was about to use, but in this real moment in time, and in a flash, I would recognize the harm or unease to the person to whom I was speaking just before the words left my lips. And in that split second, I would hold my tongue, and in the next moment, I changed the words I was about to use to words that were more productive. I called this one "Hold your tongue."

And finally, and in real time, while having conversations with someone, mind would reveal to me in a flash that the words to flow from my mouth toward the end of my sentence, words not yet in my awareness, are going to be perceived by the listener in a negative light. In that moment in time, I would get a glimpse of the real impact of those yet to be spoken words. And in the next moment, I would speak words that were more fruitful— all in the same moment and without a pause. This could seem as if I was involved in four things simultaneously—speaking, mindfully realizing harm, feeling the impact to the other party, and finding and speaking more impactful words—all in a single breath and without a pause. That is so, but it is not magic, for when we are in touch with spirit, everything becomes possible. I call this one "Spirit in motion."

When such things percolate in your life, realize that you have become immersed in consciousness, where spontaneous activities of spirit become common. This is wisdom taking form. And wisdom will become your teacher in transcending other debris from ego mind. Like anything else that we perfect, this requires patient practice and commitment. When you begin to experience heightened awareness and become dedicated to remaining in its rouse, then your commitment to self-reflection should be an effortless obligation. Make your journey a ritual. Meditate every day, and do your self-reflection and journaling every day, and this will keep you in the light of consciousness. Now lets use self-reflection to remold ourselves into divine light, moving us from the past into the present.

From Darkness to Light

Self-reflection can be used to unlock the knowing of who we are in this moment. It is looking back to observe, to question, and to examine how we came to be who we think we are. There is an idiom that says there are always three of us: the person we think we are, the person others think we are, and the person we really are. And never the twain shall meet. Which one is the true us?

Self-reflection will unfold what has been folded away and accepted, most often, unconsciously. What is our character and what are the things that formed our character? Were they positive affirming traits or were they negative and unconscious follies? Our actions and the way we present ourselves come from our motives. What are the motives that drive us, and what is the sanctity, or lack thereof, from whence they came? This exercise will bring us into a conscious state of knowing who we are, and the why of it. This is a hill we must conquer on our way to our transformation. What changes are needed for our transformation, and who will we become afterward?

Transformation is moving from the old to the new. A flowering will take place inside us, and we will become more stable, more aware, and more true to and about ourselves. We will understand how easily the simple mind distorts things and how readily it accepts things that are detrimental to our being, which is who we are, the choices we make, and the aftermath of those choices. We will understand that our unconscious internal dialogue accepts, creates, and molds us into acceptance of the person we become. Through our earthly experiences, opportunities come to us to foster change, but our unconscious frame of mind has us miss them. Self-reflection will bring a deeper awareness of the workings of the mind and the importance of knowing how to look inside to see what needs to be released. Our knowledge of honing ourselves will grow.

Who are we now, in this moment? As previously mentioned, most people are a creation of their past. Let's go back into the past to ascertain how we became the person we are today. What things shaped our thoughts, habits, and beliefs? What stories did we hold true about ourselves that may still resonate as truth to us even now? The intent of this exercise is to make true the following statement—"I am not who I was yesterday"—and bring us fully into the now, where we can make changes relative to our broader awareness of life and ourselves.

Listed below are steps designed to promote the practice of getting to know the truth of who we are. We will look at the pieces of the puzzle that made us who we are, the parts that have caused us extreme joy and extreme pain, and all else in the middle. We will examine their impact on us in how we interpreted these traumas to fit our lives. What narrative did we create, and where have these deflections taken us? This exercise will be revealing to you. You will get a clear view of your unconscious posturings, the choices you made around them, and the effects they have created inside your psyche. This will bring you from the past and into the now, where you can make glorious changes to move your new more polished self into the future. The exercise will teach you how to look and how to allocate the pieces of the puzzle that is the true you. It will teach you how to begin to heal yourself. Note that this is a short exercise. There are books available on the market with far more comprehensive exercises for looking back and for formulating the self you choose to be from a conscious frame of mind.

- Look back over your life in five-year increments, starting at the age of twelve and up to your present age. If your memory of being twelve is not credible, then start at an age at which you feel comfortable for the exercise. Look at all the experiences that influenced your state of being, including your loves, your brilliance, and your natural abilities. Look at your joys and successes, your failures, and your small and very large disappointments and embarrassment.

According to Northwestern University psychology professor Dan McAdams, author of *The Redemptive Self: Stories Americans Live By,* "The stories we tell ourselves about our lives don't just shape our personalities— they are our personalities." He went on to say that personality comes in layers. The first layer is our basic character, made up of traits driven by our genetics and environment. The second layer contains things such as values and goals. The third layer is the story we tell about our lives, a sort of "cognitive script." It helps us to understand how we came to be the way we are and where we think our lives are going, giving us some sense of meaning and purpose. We are, therefore, not separate from our life story, nor are we separate from the things that have influenced and informed our lives. One could say we are our experiences and the accepted influences that we hold on to, which helps to form parts of our personality.

- For each experience above, write a few short sentences on how it affected your life. How did it alter or change who you were from the level of your personality or character? How did it alter your desires, your choices, or your direction or preferences in your life?

The basic premise is that we feel we must hold values to be able to recognize our place in society. Or we feel that we must fit in so we accept or create mental constructs deliberately or unconsciously. As a result of this desire to fit in, we develop or accept beliefs about ourselves that do not reflect the truth about us. This may mean that we have a distorted sense of our own attributes or that we have accepted some exaggerated or irrational belief unconsciously, due to incidents that left us feeling below societal norm. We tend to think that we're either much better or much worse than the norm, and when the exaggerated beliefs are negative, we tend to think that the world expects less from us so we do less in that arena. This is self-sabotage and it creates much despair and social awkwardness in us. Once these beliefs are recognized, then the healing process of bringing them into perspective can begin.

- Summarize in a few short paragraphs who you are today relative to the attributes you accepted into your life and the ones you discarded from your life.

There Are No Accidents

In your daily living thus far, you may have noticed that life is a bit like a roller coaster. Life takes us up, it takes us down, and it takes us sideways sometimes. This is for us to learn, grow, and feel the bumps to make the right changes, to observe the madness of mind and move to improve our mental state. So one could look at life as a continuous episode of learning and growing, and this continuum assumes that we are aware enough to look and recognize when change is required. For without awareness, we remain the same.

There are no accidents in life. Every mental posture you adopted throughout your childhood, adolescence, and into young adulthood was for your good. Every personality trait you appropriated was for your good; every habit you fostered was for your good. We live in a world of the coexistence of opposites—yin and yang. We would not know light if there were no dark, day without night, or good without evil. Life requires this. It is through this formula that we are able to transform ourselves, moving from weakness to strength, from mediocrity to the exceptional, and from darkness into light. We cannot become transformed without seeing or knowing both sides. During our youth, our immature minds attach themselves to certain traits, which create recklessness, immaturity and vacant habits, mind-sets, and postures. We accept things into our psyche that we don't even know are there and we wonder why life seems to move us around in circles. But look back at the difference between your teenage years and your later twenties. Psychologically, you have grown. You have naturally let go of some of the traits and habits that you once held so dear, for they no longer serve you. But what about the habits that were and still are unconscious to you? We have probably accepted our quick irritability as a part of our personality. There comes a time when these immature habits or rituals no longer serve us, for we must grow. The universe sees fit to bring situations to us that require our growth through inward looking. In our unfertile mind, these situations may resemble problems, which might cause us to fret and worry, but fret not. What we call problems are actually doors being opened, giving us the opportunity to assess inwardly what is required for us to change, alter, shift, and throw out, thus lightening our load and shifting us upward to the next phase of our development.

In my teenage years, I realized that I was shy. I didn't know exactly why, because I was good in school and had many friends, and within my group of friends, I was considered smart, ambitious, and driven. But nonetheless, I accepted that I was shy and I played the part as shy people do, by staying to the background. At twenty-one, I had completed university and started my career as an information technology analyst at one of the major banks. I quickly expressed my abilities by doing services outside my job description, such as finding ways to significantly improve efficiency and productivity in various business processes of the company.

My second promotion landed me in the computer room, where I was one of the analysts responsible for keeping the massive IBM mainframe computer systems up and running. In my third month in the computer room, I received my first review and it was a C-. I was utterly shocked. I asked my manager why. He said this: "Well, you just sit there and you don't say much, so I don't know how good you are at the job." And he was right. What I would do when system problems arose was to tell the other analysts where to look and what to do to solve the problems. I had a deep command of how the computer systems worked internally and was proficient at solving problems, sometimes even before the system would fail, but I did not want to take center stage where everyone looked to me. I preferred to stay in the back as the advisor. (And now, as I am writing this, an awareness came to mind that there was a bit of rebellion in there as well—my wanting to take responsibilities on my own terms and not on the terms of others). I later learned that the other analysts would advise the manager when the problems were solved, but they would not mention that it was me who figured out the speedy resolution.

For the first time in my life, I had felt the negative consequence of being shy, for I recognized that being shy prevented me from being seen, heard, and taken seriously. I realized that shyness made me invisible, with no voice and no power. It devastated me, and in that moment, I knew I wanted change. I went outside in the lounge where we typically have lunch and play chess. I knew, at that time of day I would be alone. The horror of not being seen or heard had created a pressure that was building inside of me. I knew I never wanted to feel this way again. As I felt the angst, tears rolled down my face and I uttered these words so that I could hear them myself: "I now understand what being shy brings. I will not be seen, heard, or taken seriously. Therefore, from this day forth, I am letting go of being shy from within me."

I spoke the words out loud, and I sat there for a while to absorb what I had just said.

Five minutes later, I went back into the computer room a changed young man. Since that day, I decided to share with others what lived inside me. I created comprehensive technical training programs to educate other techies on how to effectively and quickly solve problems inside the IBM mainframe systems; I reengineered divisions of the company, increasing efficiency and effectiveness of divisions and doubling or tripling employee productivity. I moved on to larger endeavors in other companies, managing entire data centers and gaining divisional leadership positions and becoming one of the speakers at biannual corporate meetings. Do I still feel hesitant to speak? No, I don't, because when I speak, it is important, or else I listen. I speak to encourage ideas, to bring forth newness in support of broader perspectives, and to build confidence in others.

Removing shyness is an inside job. It is an internal transformation that removes the feelings of lack, fear, and anxiety from our being; thereafter, our light will shine. None of us are born shy. We develop the lack and restrictiveness during early childhood. And since most are not aware that the shackles can be removed, they remain as their own psychological jailer for most or all of their lives.

The New, More Aware Self

Now that you have become aware of the ingredients that created the person that you have come to know, it's time to create a new you. With the knowledge you have garnered and your sharper awareness, you are better equipped to construct a stronger, more powerful and aware self from this point on into the future.

- Now create the self you want to resonate from this point forward, with your full awareness and intension. Create a ritual to hone yourself daily, to keep your awareness firmly on being the true you.

Self-reflection has set your ability to observe and perceive on higher frequencies. This has brought the answers you sought. You have improved your awareness, your insight, and your knowing. Take time regularly to practice self-awareness, to ensure the self that you think you are is the self you truly are and the self others see. This brings you into harmony with yourself. Life constantly brings challenges and experiences, and we are always shifting, always honing, adapting, growing, and moving with life.

Are You Living in the Past?

Most people live in the past and in the perceived future. Yet everything happens in the present moment. When we hold a clear space in our mind, we won't need to look for things in the past that troubled us. Using the tool of self-reflection will allow any fragmented bits inside our psyche to be imparted to us, so that we can see them and transmute or release them through our observation of them. In the practice of holding a clear mind, without any additions or subtractions to the awareness, the light of our consciousness heals and releases any irrational mental fragments, never to hamper our thoughts or behaviors again. And a clear mind becomes the awareness itself. We will find we have new habits—good habits. We will realize that the work we have been doing has taken effect and that our awareness continues to expand. Things that would typically trouble us will have no further effect on us. Past ills have been replaced with "soul food"—stillness, alertness, peace, love, and reverence to all other souls. We are being transformed. We are entering the gate of the divine.

Cultivating More Space

We must become purposeful in cultivating space in our daily living. Observe the things that bog your mind, the things that trouble you even without provocation. Be easy on yourself and stay alert.

When a thought has come to an end, set it free.

Retire when the work is complete.

At the completion of an argument, release and let it be.

When a decision has been made, be still.

Row your boat with humility.

Take responsibility for what you are feeling.

Make your inner light your guide.

We must come to know when things are finished and let them go. When something annoys you with people or things, just pay attention to the feelings or the physicality in your body. Become aware of the "what is happening" and "the where in your body" it is happening, but without judgment. Watch, and allow the paradox to be exactly as it is, then let it go. When a situation arises in which you would fervently retort, remain silent and listen to, or watch, your thoughts. From that silent place inside, ask the awareness whether or not you should respond. If in the meantime you find the ego judging or interpreting, just observe it without criticism.

These are some of the daily practices for creating inner space, of unwinding the continuous strands of cobwebs that interrupt our ability to flow with consciousness. This is important in our daily living, and when we come to appreciate space, there is inward silence. It comes naturally as we observe and investigate. Then there is no division between daily living and inner silence. Silence becomes *sacred,* and the mind becomes *sacred.* This opens the door to immeasurable sacredness, which affects our daily living, such as how we think and how we talk to and treat others. Our thoughts, behaviors, maturity of love for ourselves and others, compassion, and caring can begin to take form. We are making marked progress.

Being One with Life

During meditation, we come to understand our selves at a level we could not have imagined, causing us to recognize the profound cloud of darkness and ignorance we lived in when we were unconscious. Now we recognize that this has always been our primary journey here on earth: to know whom we are, embrace who we are, and live in the sacredness of who we are. Getting to know and understand who we are facilitates the understanding of others. Meditation immerses us in the understanding of who we are and bathes us with knowledge and wisdom. It settles the divide between what is happening on the inside and the outside, which when left unnoticed is the root of our problems. Meditation raises our energy frequency. We are at a higher level of mind and recognize that during and after meditation we feel lighter, easier, and more stable from the center. Fussiness and agitations begin to fall away and no longer ail us. We refrain from the constant questioning and searching for answers. Our perception recognizes faults and misunderstandings and we simply discard them—no arguments, no insults, and no blame. We no longer need to question, doubt, or become troubled, for we just know. We are living from the center, the place of power and balance, and where we can see the paradox of duality (opposites between two concepts) and make decisions from a higher awareness. Our awareness lifts us into a state of deeper understanding and spontaneous knowing. There is a stillness inside that pervades our being and we are becoming free. Freedom comes from within, when all our fears and illusions have disappeared. Meditation brings earnestness, and wisdom is the result. We are then released from suffering. This is change.

Transcending to Higher Dimensions

Going Beyond the Void

On an ordinary day in the fall of 2012, I left this earthly plane and transcended into what I suspect is the higher realm of awareness. I will share this experience with you now and hope that you will understand the magnificence of who we really are and where we come from. That the complexities of life as we know it are shadows relative to the infinite possibilities that exist in the heart of infinity.

I left my home in Toronto on a rainy and dark evening and drove to Mississauga for my first visit to a spiritual meet-up group. At this point, I had been on the spiritual path for over fourteen years. I arrived at the community center and quickly found the room where the event was being held. There were six of us present. We quickly learned that we had all shared similar life experiences. We all felt as if our level of awareness was outside what is referred to as "human consciousness." We never did quite fit into what seemed normal for others.

We agreed that being aware was a walk that bore some moments of feeling out of place and alone. We had all realized, early in life, that we felt different but were unsure what to do about it. The room fell into a hush as we listened to each other and realized a oneness among ourselves. As the evening progressed, the leader asked about our abilities to quickly slip into the meditative zone. I mentioned that I could slip into the void in a matter of seconds. His next statement was profound to me. He said, "Entering the void is really just the shallow end. You must go beyond the void." I was a bit perplexed since I had never heard that before, yet an intrigue stayed within my awareness. The meeting was sincerely a pleasure. We all felt lucky to have met each other, due to our striking similarities.

Three days later, I was at a friend's home. This friend has attained enlightenment and our energies seem to go higher whenever we occupy the same space. We are both very inquisitive in our wanting to know the intricacies of life and trying to understand the particles and sub-particles of our being here on earth. At some point, she asked which gurus I listen to on a regular basis and what modalities I used to gain deeper awareness. She then asked if I had ever listened to Sri Nisargadatta Maharaj. I said no. She went to her computer and sent a link to my e-mail and advised me to listen to his talk when I returned home.

The next morning, I opened the link she had sent. The guru's voice was faint and his Indian accent was not making it easy for me to understand him properly, but in straining my hearing to pick up what he was saying, this statement came across loud and clear: "You must go beyond the void." I sat motionless for a minute. I realized that this was the second time in five days that I had heard this statement. I was consciously aware enough to know there are no accidents. I immediately stopped the video and decided to meditate. Typically, I meditate by sitting on the floor with my legs crossed, and usually after one hour my legs cramp and I have to come out of meditation. On this particular occasion, I decided to lie in bed. This was the first time I meditated while lying down, and you will see the significance of this at the end of my experience. I wish to note as well that there are no words in the English language, or earthly statements, that can properly express the gravity of the experience I am about to share with you. I will choose my words carefully so that you can feel the substance of the experience.

As usual, I sank into the void within seconds, enveloped by the purity of stillness, peace, and bliss, and after a few moments, I mentally stated, "Take me beyond the void." Then I remained in the stillness of the moment.

Suddenly, I was somewhere. I was alive but not alone. I was a part of something that seemed to be everlasting, which stretched through the entirety of galaxies. It was everywhere, pervasive, and powerful beyond anything the mind could comprehend. I was nowhere, yet I was everywhere. I was empty, yet I knew everything. I was in touch with everything that there is and could see beyond time and space. The feeling of being everywhere and yet never moving nor transitioning to other realms was daunting. I remained in the massiveness of this thing; it was the deepest peace, tranquility, and aliveness and I had never known it existed. These feelings were light years deeper, wider, and beyond what our earthly mind can grasp. The radiance of this thing was enigmatic, deeply alluring, beyond intense, and hypnotic. Yet I could not stop looking, feeling, and radiating in cosmic bliss. It glittered in colors that moved through each other, creating shattering shades that cannot be described—the beauty and vibrancy of which drew me in. I was a part of it and it was a part of me. The intensity of love was like one million volts of electricity moving through me, but with a magnetic sweetness beyond words. It felt as nurturing as home, secure, alive, everlasting, perpetual, and forever. I continued looking, feeling, and being with it. This uninterrupted field of bliss, of nothingness, was alive and it was conscious. And I was a part of it.

I remained consciously aware that this was happening, although I could not fathom any of it, and in the utmost stillness of mind, I decided to mindfully ask this everlasting entity a question: "Where am I and what is this that I am a part of?" The answer came in the form of brimming bold words, and the words seem to fall heavily into my being, resonating into and through me like heavy electricity and then evaporating into my entire consciousness: my cells, molecules, atoms, skin, bones, mind, brain—everything. "You are God" was the response.

As the words fell heavily into my being a clear understanding followed. This understanding felt more like flickering shadows of radiant light that also settled into me, becoming a part of me, never to be removed. The understanding was that all of us come from this place, this thing. I understood that all of us, in spirit, make up what we refer to as God, the absolute, the all-knowing, omnipotent. This understanding also included beings from other worlds, planets, and systems where souls take on some form or another. I understood the extent and completeness and vastness of God, of the universe, of everlasting, expanding without end. It was all inside me now. This was a "happening" from which there is no returning to my prior self.

The indelible mark left from this experience is total and absolute and permanent. My next question was "If I am here, how can I be on earth as soul?" Again the answer was powerful, pervasive, and immediate. The response was "You have never left here. No one ever leaves here. It is only the dust, a tiny essence of spirit, that goes to earth as soul, and through soul, you are always connected to spirit, which is who you are." The understanding that followed was this: When we pray to God, we are speaking to spirit, which is our self in God. Our soul has a direct link to spirit that is in God; therefore, we are always connected to God through soul. We are, therefore, never alone. I remained in this state of grace for a while, and suddenly, I was back in my bedroom. It felt as if a half hour had passed, but when I looked at the clock, five hours had elapsed. Time had stood still.

This experience has marked me with a knowing of who we truly are, and I knew I would never be the same again. For now there is neither thinking nor wondering about who we are or where we come from. There is no speculation as to whether or not there is something out there, something that is the spearhead of our expanding universe and something from which come the laws of the universe. The knowing sank into my being and cannot ever be removed. Now I know and that knowledge has married me to truth, to aliveness and to my conviction to play my part in the evolutionary process called life, in this time, on planet earth.

A spontaneous act of divine grace took place, one for which I can only move forward. Life has never been the same for me. I see God everywhere. I see God through the eyes of others. I sense God in the essence surrounding others. I feel God in the hearts of some. I know God through a smile or a gentle nod. I see beauty in everyone. I feel consciousness everywhere.

I know I am never alone—none of us are ever alone. I have learned to speak to myself, my higher self, when I need answers or direction. The self responds in kind and love always and the answers are immediate and spacious. I feel and acknowledge guidance from within, for I know who I am and where I come from. I am forever changed.

The Absolute

Going beyond the void is the beginning and the end of all there is. Understand that the "I" is the unified field of existence, and the "I" requires the paradox of duality on planet earth. The "I" is life and all its manifestations and knowledge. The "I" acquires and sustains memory. The "I" is time bound and includes birth, death, and being. The "I" is a part of this world, but realize that we are more than a cog in the unified field of existence. We transcend birth and death and time, and karma. We are prior to the "I."

You are man, you are God, you are consciousness, you are substance, and you are intelligent. Gain the knowledge of whom you are through meditation by allowing the seeker to disappear. Then you will know that you are the absolute. You are the all in all, for the creator and the created are ONE.

—Sri Nisargadatta Maharaj

Eminence of Higher Dimensions

The act of transcending to higher dimensions in this particular modality was spontaneous, a flowering of grace from the divine. While it may not happen for everyone, it is worth trying to apply the technique for "going beyond the void." We are infinite beings with infinite possibilities. I have added one other technique below that describes how to journey to higher dimensions. I sincerely hope that you garner the courage to take the leap, for it will allow you to know, at the deepest level of your being, that you are infinite.

We are spiritual beings in a human body, embedded in this fourth-dimensional space-time continuum called earth. Yet our spiritual essence is eternal and constant and defies both time and space. During and after our transcendent journey to higher dimensions, our consciousness will shift. It has no choice, because we have experienced something beyond the limits of our imagination, something our mind could not have fathomed. Through such experience, the mind now sees and knows. The mind evolves, and our conscious awareness therefore follows suit. We have been raised from our physical base, earth, to higher frequencies, which raise our level of consciousness accordingly. The higher consciousness we experienced will be brought back with us into our physical life. Our frequency and our level of consciousness have been permanently raised; we will notice that we possess a different mind-set, a very different perspective on life. We will feel the reality of God and the actuality of infinity; we will relish our commune with nature, and we will do it often. We will realize that it is the soul that traveled to higher dimensions, for our body remained where it was during our travel; therefore, we discover for the first time that our soul is real and it is conscious. Our awareness will be at a higher state of absolute knowing; we will possess divine wisdom where questions are generally not necessary; and we will often experience subtle moments of bliss. This aliveness paves the way for the rest of our spiritual journey as we look forward to further experiences in dimensions or worlds outside the bounds of earth. We no longer wonder about the infiniteness of the universe, for we have experienced a slice of time and space without end.

Take the seat of asana, the seat for meditation. Relax, and just follow the breath, allowing it to flow on its own terms. Pay attention to the rise and fall of the stomach on each inhalation and exhalation. Just follow the breath, until the breath vanishes. Feel the gentle vibrations inside your body, the space that surrounds you. It is around and through you. You are immersed in it. Recognize the feelings that are percolating through you: feelings of love, joy, peace, and harmony. Feel all that there is. Feel the effortlessness of "being" and the inherent power. Just feel. You are in the void. With love, simply ask to be taken beyond the void and relax into the knowing that you have been heard.

Out-of-Body Experience (OBE)

Thought is one of the most powerful vibrations in the universe. Although our thoughts, here on earth, do not immediately create the objects of our thought, this is due to the extreme denseness of earth's vibration and the fickleness and wavering of the mind. In higher dimensions, our thoughts instantly create the objects of our thought. The purpose of out-of-body experiences is to move us to higher dimensions, into higher vibratory frequencies and realities, moving through far less dense cores of the universe to experience other worlds and to experience our true self without a dense body.

The nature of reality is consciousness. We are that consciousness and that is all we are. That's what we take with us wherever we go—consciousness. We are pure creativity and can connect to our own potential to create, including the creation of our own realities through thought. The OBE expands the mind, bringing immediate shifts in consciousness that broaden the understanding of the nature of reality, accelerating the process of expanding our awareness of consciousness. We are consciousness creating our realities through thought response. When it comes to other dimensions, science is limited. There is an endless series of dimensions and, therefore, an unlimited number of firsthand experiences for us to have. All higher dimensions are far less dense than earth and are "thought responsive." This means that anything we think can be instantly manifested. It's important to be aware that when we transcend earth via OBE, we take our state of consciousness with us. That is, our fears, anxieties, and even elements from past lives. But this is good, for OBE causes us to confront our fears without trauma. We can, therefore, confront our issues in a nonthreatening way. We can heal our earthly issues more rapidly, since we are closer to source and can advance our personal evolution to all that is part of us. OBE provides a much greater opportunity to heal on all levels, and transformation or spiritual awakening can occur more readily.

My experiences with leaving this planet were not planned. I was surprised but not shocked. After the automobile accident in 1998, my business as a project management consultant in the high-tech industry came to an abrupt end. With my brain not fully functional, and my memory still gravely erratic at best, I had little choice. In 2000, I created my own product invention and engineering firm. I felt that inventing was something I could do, even if the functionality of my brain was still wavering. I thought I would start in the toy industry, because through my initial investigations, it seemed that they use inventors for some of their new products. I say "seemed" because that was not as true as I thought. In fact, the business of product inventions is one in which inventors are set up to be taken advantage of by larger companies, but since I was not one who was easily frightened by what may happen, I created four toy concepts and went off to an Inventors Forum Showcase in Las Vegas.

This was one of the largest shows for all the major and midsize toy developers and retailers from North America. The inventors were set up in a very large room, with approximately 150 booths of new inventions. Toy-industry speakers organized their talks to give us, the inventors, a view of the industry as it related to new trends, as well as to the state of the industry as a whole. It was great to listen to these talented men, but one gentleman caught my attention. Harry had just left the post as president of one of the larger toy suppliers in the United States. He was one of the most brilliant minds I have ever heard, and he was quite funny too. I felt a natural pull toward him and hoped to meet him one-on-one.

But who said there is no magic? For magic happened a few hours later. After all these geniuses had a look through all the inventions, I was summoned to a one-on-one with Harry. He advised me to pack up my booth and travel, one week later, to his home in the Adirondacks. "Why do I need to pack?", I asked. He stated that all the geeky guys walking beside presidents and vice presidents were there to steal ideas. Even though we had just met, there was a sincere respect between us. I did what he asked. I packed up during lunch and left the Forum.

Several days later, I packed my prototypes and drove to his home to meet him. As it happens, it was fall season, and the sight of the Adirondacks was spectacular. His home resided in the foothills of the mountain, so the drive up the mountain was no less than epic. I was thrilled.

We sat at his dining table and forged a partnership. I was to continue to create fresh new products, starting with the ones I had already created, and he would advise which toy company would be best to approach with each. He himself would be the contact to get my products into any and all of the top companies, beginning with Toys R Us. The deal was set so I came back to Toronto to truly begin the process of creating "the first of their kind" products for the toy industry. This included developing each concept into a fully functional, working prototype to prove the technology works and developing a "story" for the products, signifying the "why" of the products. I was born with an inventive mind, so I knew well the capabilities of mind and that mind would travel, if necessary, to other worlds or other dimensions and bring back new insights for my eyes only. What I did not expect was that mind would take me alongside itself.

So there I was, standing in a world that was not earth, on the shore of what looked like an ocean, somewhat similar to earth's but different too. The water ebbed and flowed with denseness, a thickness, moving more like soup. There in front of my eyes, images, like that of a jigsaw puzzle, began to formulate, being put together as I looked on. The parts were moving and shifting into form and out of form, with a new formula of design on each turn. This continued until the object was fully assembled in midair, as if the atmosphere had hands, eyes, and thought.

Something else of interest is that the image and the precise details of its features would remain solidly in my mind until such a time it was completely assembled in physical form here on earth. At this point, the details would disappear from my mind, leaving only remnants of it. The mechanics of the technology and engineering to be used were also planted in my psyche. What was also interesting was that when dealing with engineers with regard to building prototypes, they would tell me that there was no technology to accurately satisfy the functionality of these products. At that point, I would relay the information on the technology to be used, which was most often the coupling of two or more different technologies. Once the engineers attempted it, they would call me with utter surprise, asking how I knew that. They wanted to know, but I did not tell. I didn't think they would understand.

I have been to a world where the valleys were picturesque with plants, shrubbery, and trees all moving together like the waves of sound created by a symphony. In one particular instance, I was looking across a meadow adjacent to rolling hills and valleys. I saw an interesting tree in the distance that drew my attention. I thought that I would like to be sitting underneath that tree, but getting there would take some time. In the next moment, I was sitting under that tree. What I had thought was manifested in the next moment.

OBE changes you. A new world opens up. Your mind expands, creating significant shifts in consciousness. It brings a much broader understanding of the nature of reality. There are no illusions in higher dimensions like the illusions on planet earth. And these experiences can move the nonbelievers into spirituality, because once you have seen and experienced truth, you cannot return to your previous state in which you lacked this understanding or were ignorant of this knowledge. With OBE, truth does not change. You discover truth through your own profound experiences by exploring beyond the physical. And in that place, there are no man-made beliefs, religions, or science to affix oneself to. Therefore, this is the path to truth. This is all we have to experience—our true self. When the human body dies on earth, the soul simply transitions to another level of consciousness. It either goes home or to whatever world it is transitioned to, and there are a myriad of possibilities.

OBE is spiritual exploration through which we accelerate our personal development. The mind is expanded into an area of who we truly are. This is solid proof that we are not our possessions, nor our ego or our body. True learning is to consciously evolve through experiencing what we wish to learn. We experience our true self, which is a multidimensional being, and we quickly become aware of the continuation of life after the body dies and know that we are immortal.

> We are beyond mind, intellect, cause, and effect.
> We are beyond linear time.
> We are beyond the universe.

This brings part 1 of the book to a close.

In Part 1, we learned how to move past fear. We established methods through which to allocate the "self" by quieting the simple mind. And by going deeper inside, through meditation, we were able to feel and know our true self. Through continued meditation, we have gone deeper within and recognized our true essence, and we have felt the nature of pure peace. We have learned that through OBE, our spirit self can move about without the human body, and this in itself will significantly broaden our awareness about our true self.

Part 2 focuses on getting to know who we are at the deepest level of our being. It reveals the unraveling of the bondage that placates this place called earth. It equips us with the tools to release the bondage, so that we can transcend the ego mind, move deeper into higher mind, the mind of the soul, and regain the clarity of our true self. It allows us to know the inherent power we wield for ourselves and for humanity. As our awareness grows, we gain wisdom and feel the oneness of this unitary force. We know that we are bound as one and must function as one for the plight of humanity.

We will learn the system of energy that we are and the mechanics to heal the body and mind. We will learn that we are living in the physical world and the spirit world all at once. We will see that the things we think and do, and who we become, affect us in both worlds at once. We will learn the intricacies of our energy system and how to regulate our body, both the physical and the subtle bodies, through kriya/kundalini yoga, and through pranayama controlled breathing via the movement of prana, the universal energy that is our life force. We will explore the subconscious mind to locate wounds that were unconscious to us and learn how to heal them by removing them permanently. We will understand what the soul is, who we truly are, and move through the process to redeem the soul. We will become aligned with our true self in readiness to merge body, mind, and soul to gain our salvation through deeper spiritual awakening.

Healing

Preparing the Body

A System of Energy

We are a continuum of probability shrouded in an infinite field of potentiality, existing at the junction between spirit and matter. We are living within a world of form, and in a world of no form between the physical and the nonphysical, living in an ocean of pure consciousness, pure potential. We live in, and are a part of the prevalent energy that regulates our lives. Everything is energy: our thoughts, feelings, emotions, and perceptions. The constant movement of these energies through the body, or the restriction of the movement of these energies through the body, brings to us our mental welfare, our liveliness, and our behaviors and attitudes.

It is imperative that we become aware of the energy system that we are. We are a vessel that receives energy from the cosmos and transforms it into food to restore and regulate the body to form, function, and aliveness. When energy flow is unencumbered, life is good. We are healthy and our complex system is working effortlessly; our emotional, mental, and psychological well-being remains intact. However, negative energy can be exhausting and cause our emotional state to become out of alignment. If we expend energies by indulging in fruitless mind stuff, our complex system can be thrown off course. The inherent result can and does include the slowing or depletion of the flow of energy through the body. When energy is depleted, the results cast unwanted effects on the body, effects that we may feel immediately, such as emotional or physical drain or discomfort.

However, that's just the beginning. Depletion of energy causes the body to become vulnerable to many other negative effects. This can include the creation of blockages and the formation of disease. Blockages are formed from energies that become stuck in the cells and organs of the body, the root of which are negative emotions, typically produced by stress. This stress can come in the form of fear, anxiety, guilt, shame, or depression.

Blockages also occur when there is an energy bleed from the body. This happens when there is repeated negative emotional bedlam. Any lack of cosmic energy inside the human body is cause for dysfunction, leading to various misalignments and ending with mental, psychological, emotional, or physical ailments. Our overall well-being therefore, is largely dependent on our mental and emotional state. Many things contribute to this state: how we feel, about ourselves; how we feel about others; how we resolve conflicts; who we are from the inside; our perceptions; the things we hold on to; and our unconscious beliefs, fears, and stresses. All of which echoes who we are being right now, not from the level of personality but from the substance of who we are on the inside, in this moment. Everything matters in the now.

How do we know if we have blockages? A very broad clue is trying to manifest our desires, whether it is starting a new business, getting a promotion, or some movement of progress we wish to make. We realize that the immediate response from our awareness is a feeling of unworthiness or lack. The subconscious mind stands between our desires and us. It will let us know through feelings of "not being good enough," through our resistance to achieving a goal, through our fear of success, and through our perceived consequences of successfully achieving an objective, that we have negative subconscious content. These are blockages. Any feelings of lack, such as the inability to believe in and trust ourselves regarding our success, may have already been implanted within our subconscious from early childhood years or through present-moment unconscious beliefs. Removing blockages clears our communication pathway to universal intelligence and improves our meditation, concentration, visualization, and creativity.

How do we go about creating a healthy emotional well-being? This chapter will provide enlightenment through content on how blockages occur and their effects on our energy system: the body, our emotions, and our spiritual, psychological, and physical well-being. Remedies are provided on how to keep our system in a healthy state of being and how to get ourselves back in a state of "flow" after recognizing the blockages. Use the exercises to create daily rituals and to keep your energy system in perfect alignment.

The Subtle Body System

Chakras

Science has recently discerned the complexity of the one life that all humans share and is still trying to assess the part each human plays in this pervasive consciousness throughout time and space. Science now understands the oneness that is life—a culmination of all that there is: sun, moon, stars, trees, water, plants, and man; everything is alive. The spectrum of what we call humankind is more complex than one would suspect. We are a sophisticated energy system intricately put together and plotted with precision, with the accuracy for what we have come here to experience and influence: life. We are perfect in our design and makeup, and as we continue to evolve with life, life itself, continues to expand, shift, and evolve.

We are comprised of a column of energy with several centers, each with its own series of characteristics and particular functions for our expansion and evolution. Each directs our well-being toward our emotions, our manifestations, and our awakening. Seven main chakras form our system of energy, and proper alignment of these chakras is key to the fulfillment of our lives. Chakras take energy from the cosmos, from spirit, and transform it into matter, our body. In essence, the chakras act as the interface adapters anchoring our body to the world.

These centers can become blocked for various reasons, and when they do, they lose energy, as you would lose blood. When, for example, you are under stress, you can actually feel the depletion of energy in your body. This loss of energy can and does cause your body to function inefficiently, opening you up to a variety of discomforts, illness, and disease. These centers are located in our esoteric or spirit body, but their effects are felt within the physical body. When chakras become misaligned, the effects manifest in either of two ways: as disease in the physical body or as psychological problems that pounce on you throughout your life. When properly aligned, the power and vibration in these centers increase and your life works in proper order; everything feels good and is good. Through these centers, energies manifest as matter. The unseen becomes the visible; desires are attained; tasks and ventures are accomplished with ease. Chakras are therefore our direct conduit through which we experience life.

Chakras are most susceptible during the early childhood years. Blockages occur easily as a child develops immature beliefs or assumptions and holds emotional distress due to negative incidents when they feel lack in one or more areas of their lives. Or simply, anything that places a strain upon their psyche can cause blockages. They carry their karma and other psychological baggage with them from previous incarnations, and they develop anxieties from not feeling loved, nurtured, or encouraged during the developmental years. This restricts the flow of energy to and from the chakras.

Chakras are our emotional compass, each radiating the motion or movement of energy that corresponds to its function. When an experience occurs in the body, the corresponding chakra allows us to feel the vibratory frequency of the emotion generated from that experience. A high frequency, such as the feelings of love, carries a strong energy pattern. Conversely, a low frequency, which includes negativity in any form, carries a weak energy pattern and can and does disrupt the chakras, taking them out of balance.

Awareness is extremely important in keeping our inner systems intact. In other words, block nothing. Whenever we are experiencing any emotion in the body, just feel it. For example, when the feeling of jealousy comes up, do not ignore it. Feel it. When we block the feeling, we are blocking the experience in the now, and in so doing, we are blocking the flow of energy to and from the chakras. The results will be clogged or stagnant chakra with stale energy, and this can cause the chakras to spin irregularly or become distorted or torn. When the chakras are functioning normally, each one will be open and spinning properly to metabolize the particular energies needed from the universal energy field. Our health and well-being are dependent upon allowing our system to perform its function as we become the awareness behind the experiences. Remember we are here to experience life, so open up to all experiences. Experiencing is living.

The Awareness

If you were to completely think thoughts of love and assurance, your body's energy would flow smoothly in and through the chakras. You would no doubt feel happy and healthy. On the other hand, fearful thoughts negatively affect your chakras' ability to function. They cause the chakras to become dirty, shrunken, or swollen. That is why you may feel out of sorts or lethargic and not understand why. Obsessive thoughts cause the chakras to become enlarged and twist out of proportion. When there is an energy imbalance in the chakras, the chakras tend to close down, starting at the crown and moving downward to the root.

We must become more effective at managing our emotional well-being, and this can be done not through our immediate reactions to what we perceive as a negative polarity but through recognition of the present emotion. Simply engage the observer, notice the emotion, and bear the feelings of the emotion, without becoming wholly engaged in the emotion. Notice the emotion and allow it to run its course without adding anything to it or subtracting anything from it. Do not become physically engaged with it. In other words, watch the emotion with complete detachment, as you would watch your children playing a sport they love. Just watch and observe in the stillness of mind. For example, when someone expresses his or her love for you, your fourth chakra increases its rotation and this is felt as the "love" emotion in the heart region. Simply feel the emotion. Nothing else is necessary in that moment.

If you are feeling a perceived negative emotion and buy into the emotion by accepting it as truth, you are now vulnerable. Your chakra will flow out of balance and you have created a blockage. If it is a fear that arises, simply watch the fear with detachment as the observer. Chakras misfire when we lean into what they are showing us with negativity, and attaching negativity to any flow of energy will cause imbalance and blockages.

We have choices. We can watch and allow the emotion to flow fully to its completion, or we can watch it with detachment. Do not try to suppress the emotion or disown it or become entangled in it such that you lose your present-moment awareness. We must deal with the emotion as it happens, right now, in this moment.

When you are consciously aware and can simply watch the emotion, it completes itself and no blockages occur. You receive the lesson to be learned from the emotion, or you experience the joy brought on by the emotion and the full awareness is received. In this way, the chakra remains healthy and intact. You are secure in sustaining your awareness in the now. This is good.

When you do this, your world will reveal itself to you. Know that everything in this universe is in perfect order. When an emotion arises, gaze wholeheartedly into the emotion to see the reason or the purpose for it. The realization is the seed to your highest growth and to your deeper feelings and accomplishments, and healing takes place. This is the practice of liberating yourself.

Soul incarnated with specific energy patterns through which to experience a particular flavoring of life. Each experience is ours alone. The important thing is for us to identify what the experience is telling us, so that we can learn and grow from it. We are at the helm. We steer the ship of our life. Therefore, participate in the knowledge of how the system, that is our body, works in accordance with the movement of energy. Take charge and hone the realities for the life you are leading. Understand that emotions do not show up to hurt or bruise us but to advise us. They are our beacons. Search vehemently for what they want to reveal to you and receive deeper insight and wisdom. Your life will flourish.

Unblock Past Blockage

The way to alleviate emotional blockages is to go back into the past and reenact the situation so the emotions are back in the present moment. Don't be afraid or intimidated by them. Bring them into the light of your consciousness, and let them flow unencumbered. Feel the emotions, and take full responsibility, but do not become entangled in the story and create any judgments, or else you will recreate the emotional wound. Let the emotions (energies) flow. Forgive yourself if it is required and then let go. Breathe. It is done. The emotions will flow right through your energy system (chakras) and out of your energy field. The chakras will become clear and pure again.

As was previously stated, we are born with emotional and psychological baggage from previous incarnations, so how do we alleviate these blockages?

There came a time some years ago when I felt as if I was on the verge of another vibrational shift. Thus far, I had always felt when a shift was imminent, and then at some point the shift would occur. You don't know it in the moment that it is happening. You become aware that it has happened only afterward, through feelings of freshness, lightness, and being unclogged. Life feels easy, and you feel grateful. And then comes the awareness that a subtle shift in consciousness has taken place. During this particular period, I had been feeling a shift coming on for some time, but as time passed, it still did not materialize. Even more time elapsed and still nothing, until the awareness came that I may be blocking my own evolution. I pondered for many days, and then weeks, on what habit or trait or obsession I needed to let go, but nothing came. I decided to ask for help. I called a friend who is a healer/psychic. I have known other psychics, but this friend seemed to have direct access to more information than any other psychic I have known. She has an immense connection to something out there, for she is never wrong. I called her and booked an appointment, and when the day came, I went to see her.

We said our hellos and I took my seat. She closed her eyes and went into her world, and after a few seconds, she spoke. "Yes," she said, "there is something that you are holding on to from the past."

And after a few more seconds, she said, "But it's not from this lifetime; it's from a past life."

I was shocked, for up to this point, I did not know that past-life stuff could travel with souls into other incarnations. But in order not to interrupt her connection and flow, I kept silent.

After a few moments, and with eyes still closed as if watching a movie from behind her eyelids, she said, "Oh, here it is. You are carrying a very deep guilt from a past life."

"Oh," she continued, "you have been carrying this for some time."

In a previous lifetime and at the age of nine years, I was by the seashore with my best friend who was also nine. We were on a concrete walkway alongside the ocean and we were both quite mischievous. We wanted to jump into the water—boys will be boys. He asked me to jump first, and I asked him to go first. This went on for a bit, as it happens with kids. Here was the clincher: my psychic friend informed me that I traveled in all lifetimes with an excellent command of whatever language or languages I spoke. That command allows me to easily convince others to see things my way. "And I could do this even at the tender age of nine years?" I asked.

She said yes.

So in essence, I convinced him to jump first, and he did. I was expecting him to jump in feet first, but he jumped in headfirst. The tides in that area were shallow at the time. He broke his neck and died. Now comes the magic: As she was relaying this event to me, I remembered. I remembered the entire thing. As the memories rolled through me, I saw and felt the entire thing all over again. The tears came again in the here and now. In a sense, I was in three places at once. I was standing there along the water's edge as my present adult self, watching this event happen all over again, with my heart breaking into many pieces. I was also in the "now" of 2010, sitting in my friend's living room, watching and feeling the event through vivid memory. And in both places, I was crying profusely and feeling the heaviness of my heart breaking. Inside this time and space, I had also been taken back in time, being reconnected with my nine-year-old self and was right there, seeing and feeling the trauma of my friend's death in the here and now, in the present moment.

As the tears poured out, my friend (the psychic) advised me that this is the problem that I have been carrying with me all this time. She advised that I must release the shame and guilt, and I must do it now.

"How do I do that?" I asked.

"Just say the words, and then let it go," she replied.

So with tears still pouring and my heart pounding in my chest, I uttered, "I here and now release this shame and guilt from my energy field."

With eyes still closed, I imagined the dark energies leaving my body. Perhaps several minutes elapsed in pure silence, and thereafter, I opened my eyes and felt easy. I felt free. It was done.

Allow me to elaborate on two insights. The first is this: It may not be entirely true that our memories from past incarnations are erased when we reincarnate. Our wounds, traumas, and mind-related issues are stored in our subconscious and carried into our present incarnation. This makes it possible for us to access any subconscious wounds from past lifetimes. However, if content from a past life comes into one's awareness, it may not register with their knowing or their memory in this lifetime; thus, the memory may be confusing to them. For this reason, the help of past-life regression healers may be required to assist in accessing and releasing "subconscious wounds" that may include blockages from previous lifetimes.

The second is this: When you are in the act of releasing "subconscious blockages," whether from past or present lifetimes, remember without a doubt that you are spirit. Whatever you speak aloud or with your strong intention, it is done. Do not concern yourself with thoughts about whether or not it is going to happen. When you hold a definitive state of knowing that it is done, then so shall it be. Become keenly acquainted with the fact that we are spirit and spirit has the commanding power to do anything it wishes.

Emotions come from our experiences. Ask yourself as much as possible, "What am I feeling now?" Take charge and become responsible for what you are feeling. Feelings are your internal guide, and your awareness is paramount. You and you alone must become the gatekeeper for what is happening inside you in the now as well as what is happening in your outer life. Gain success in managing your emotions. When you can accomplish this, you will naturally learn to love yourself.

A Defense Mechanism

Childhood is a vulnerable time for humans. An unborn child can feel his or her mother's emotions, which if negative can affect the child emotionally. The years from zero to eight are critical since any shock from parents or society can result in emotional scars that could become permanent. At birth, the crown, third-eye, and throat chakras are open, but they close up by age three to protect the child from severe emotional tugs.

During the teenage years, it is the heart chakra and the solar plexus chakra that become vulnerable. The heart chakra closes through rejection from parents or from a lost love. The solar plexus chakra becomes vulnerable due to the pressure to fit in and to do things we don't want to. By the time many of us reach adulthood, we have closed down all but the first two chakras (root and sacral), and even those often have imbalances due to energy blocks. Chakra closures or imbalances are caused by repetitive negative emotional sabotage. After high school, when there is usually less pressure to conform, for some, the process reverses itself and the chakras open in an upward direction, including the solar plexus, heart, and upward to the crown.

Why do we want to identify and remove energy blocks and imbalances from our chakras? It has been understood in the East for many generations that illness often manifests in the chakras before the physical body. Complete physical healing cannot take place if the chakra systems are out of balance. When there is a blockage or imbalance in one part of the chakra system, all other chakras are affected. Imbalances occur when there is too much or too little energy flowing through the chakras. The energy flowing through the chakras is prana. Prana is our life force, the energy that sustains our body and keeps us healthy and alive. When there is an imbalance of prana through the body, disease will find a way in.

By understanding how each chakra affects a particular body function and/ or life issue, it is possible to identify where a chakra is malfunctioning. Various techniques can then be used to balance the chakra system and restore physical, emotional, mental, and spiritual health to the individual. Holding negative thoughts causes the chakras to become clogged with dense, dark energy. This prevents the chakras from providing sufficient vital energy for the body. Unbalanced or blocked chakras create a whole range of mental, emotional, and physiological conditions. As mentioned previously, we incarnate with unresolved baggage from previous lifetimes. In this way, we could come into life with chakras that are already blocked. This could, in part, predetermine our attitudes and behaviors. Some therapists believe the imbalances in our chakras are influenced by both our childhood and cultural experiences. It is implied that one of the ways we try to protect ourselves is by unconsciously closing down the relevant chakra so we won't feel uncomfortable emotions. This is a defense mechanism.

Balancing Your Chakras

I am not suggesting that you learn how to unblock your own chakras. What you can do for yourself is to become consciously aware such that you don't unconsciously create blockages. There are many practitioners who can assist in rebalancing your chakras. The information below, therefore, is simply to acquaint you with some of the techniques to keep you in balance and radiate beautiful light.

Frequency

Our bodies are made up of vibrating atoms that respond to sound and colour frequencies, both of which are forms of vibrating energy. The intelligent nature of our body is to easily return to its natural state of resonance when healing energy is available. Therefore, Chakras can be brought into alignment quite readily. The optimal method is to use both colour and sound energies together since each chakra is representative of a specific tone (musical scale) and colour. These sounds directly affect the autonomic, immune, endocrine, and neuropeptide systems.

Quartz Crystals

Practitioners of alternative medicine know of the spiritual power of quartz crystals. They have the ability to cleanse negative energy and heal ailments. Quartz crystals are, therefore, some of the most common materials used for chakra balancing. Crystals focus, amplify, and change energy. When, for instance, thought energy interacts with a crystal, the thought frequencies are harmoniously changed, shifting the thought pattern and harmonics to higher vibratory frequencies. Crystals then can be used to strengthen positive intentions or affirmations. Chakra balancing should be done often to maintain proper health.

Yoga/Pranayama

Yoga brings the body, mind, and spirit into balance and into perfect alignment. This is the nature of the true self, the self we seek. Use kriya, kundalini, or pranayama exercises, to push life energy up through the chakras to make union with the crown chakra. This process forces the chakras to become open and to spin in their desired direction. It also removes rogue blockages, thus healing the body and mind and reopening the channel for pranic energy—your life force—to roam unencumbered through the body. Negative issues may be brought into your conscious awareness during this process. Your system is showing you what issues are causing the blockages. Don't participate in the memory; just become aware of them and *consciously* let them go. One very effective way to let issues go permanently is through the act of forgiveness.

Forgiveness

Forgiveness is a process unto itself, one that brings awareness, understanding, and wisdom. This is not something someone tells you to do. It is something you do for yourself, from deep within you, to relieve yourself and to heal yourself. Forgiveness will never be about the people who caused the perceived harm to you. It is about you relieving your baggage and clearing the path for your movement to higher vibrations. As the old saying goes, "People do the best with what they know at the time," so someone may not have been willfully hurting you. They were most likely ignorant of the repercussions of their actions, and if that was the case, then they meant you no harm. You can look at your pain from another viewpoint—what was done unto you was meant to be done unto you as a part of your life experience, such as having a parent who did not show you love—and you may look at this as a negative. But in the orchestration of life, you must learn through your pain to stand in the grace of your own self, with power and confidence. This means that you must go inside to garner the courage, wisdom, and strength to change yourself and your life. This is how you evolve. And in loving yourself, your salvation becomes the giver of love in whatever form or fashion you so inspire. You are healed, and your troubles become your glory. This is life.

Whatever process you use to forgive, your intention must be virtuous and pure. It cannot be a lie. Seek first the insight for what forgiveness is and what it brings. It's not just the letting go. It is about the understanding that it is absolute rubbish to blame anyone for anything that befell you.

Remember everything in this universe is perfect in its orchestration. What you look upon as an injustice is most likely the repercussion of decisions you made on the road of life that have brought you to where you are right now. Think of these ills as blessings. Find a method of forgiveness that works for you, and do it with your whole heart and full intention. The healing will occur and wisdom will follow, and it will reveal the inaccuracy in your perceptions or thought processes. We are all connected and nothing happens for naught. Your only control in this life is through the way you think and how you process the things that happen. Therefore, the greater part of your healing is the wisdom that comes from forgiveness. Wisdom will alter your method of thinking and create room for more wisdom to follow.

Qigong

Qigong is an ancient Chinese system of exercise and meditation that harmonizes the mind, body, and soul. It was inspired by the shamans, Taoists, and Buddhists, all of whom sought harmony and peace in the solitude of nature. Qigong is a spiritual discipline that cultivates peacefulness, health, and well-being. It is an efficient healing tool for balancing the energies that regulate the body.

Qi, also called chi, is our vital energy force that gives the body life. In India it is called prana, but in either case, it is our vital life force. It is the movement of this life energy flowing unencumbered through the body that is the source of our health and well-being. When there are blockages in the body that restrict the flow of qi, we suffer. How then does one protect oneself from losing or contaminating this vital energy that sustains life in the body? You do it through the regular practice of qigong.

Qigong is considered a "moving meditation" in which the breath, the body, and the mind move in synchronistic harmony. During practice, one can feel the steadiness of mind and the purity of peace from the inside out. When directed in the body with purpose, qi (energy) can cure many ailments, such as reducing chronic pain, migraine headaches, allergies, and digestive problems, as well as stopping internal bleeding and more.

Qigong can raise the testosterone level in men and balance the estrogen levels in women. It can help people with eye problems, diabetes, cancer, heart disease, and cystic fibrosis and can even help with infertility. A phrase used by my own qigong master is this: "Qigong is like acupuncture without the needles."

Qigong masters are trained healers who have mastered their discipline and who can easily detect energy blockages, even without touching the patient. During the healing process, visualization techniques are used by the qi master to establish what it is they want to accomplish at the end of the healing. That is, holding the intention of what they want to accomplish during the healing process. There are many disciplines or techniques used for moving qi through the body or directing this vital life force energy inside specific areas of the body. If the patients are aware, they can feel when the restriction in the body loosens or when it has completely vanished. Qi is available to anyone who chooses to practice often and with intention. The ardent student is asked to practice regularly to heal herself to remain in a state of flow with the vibrant energy of qi.

Is chi a revolution in medicine on the wings of ancient Chinese wisdom? The Chinese methods of healing diseases and ailments in the body remain the same today as they were over 5,000 years ago, which is by harmonizing the body with the movement of chi. Although some medical practitioners in China have adapted the Western way of healing, that of using drugs, they still use the movement of chi, herbs, needles, massage, and meditation for healing. Many who need medical help are not always looking for drugs. They are looking for other methods of assistance. Their ailments include every illness known to man. As a culture, the Chinese believe that corrective solutions to ills, whether mental or physical, are based on balancing the chi energy, which is harmonizing yin and yang. They believe the whole system of the body is based on chi.

Yin and yang were brought into being through chaos in the universe. Within everything in every part of the universe are these two opposing forces. They are interdependent and cannot exist without each other. Where one ends, the other begins, and the struggle is in maintaining the balance. We are all born in a balanced state, but we fall out of balance due to mental and psychological bedlam. Where does the body and mind fall out of balance? The answer is when there is either too much or too little yin or yang. The imbalance is what qigong masters and physicians locate and fix through acupuncture, the practice of removing blockages, or teaching the incumbent how to release the blockages using qigong/tai chi. The real achievement then is one of balance, and as you live, your thoughts, emotions, and behavior are what shape your well-being, or they change your health. Be prudent, therefore, and keep your emotions in a state of flow.

I am also a student of qigong and can tell you that it truly calms the mind and relaxes the body from the inside out. It is deep meditation, even though you move during the process. The body becomes energized with fresh energy, which you can feel. There is a quiet emanating outward that is peaceful and tranquil. Have you ever felt peace so deep you can almost touch it? It is as close to bliss as one can get. Daily practice keeps you in that space of peace and mindfulness. You become one with your systems of energy.

Reiki/Hands-On Healing

A healer may remove blockages for you, but it should be understood that if you re-indulge in the memories of the past and unconsciously encourage the same or similar emotional baggage, you have just implanted another version of the same or similar blockages into your subconscious. Instead of getting a healer to simply remove the blockages, have him/her guide you through a process of mindfully looking at your issues and, with love, letting them go. If this is done properly, you will immediately feel easy, lighter, and fresh. In this way, you will know how to remove other rogue blockages from your system. Your inner and outer world will become synchronized and the feelings of freedom will come to you naturally.

It was the fall of 2011, in the latter part of October, and I was feeling a bit unearthed. The house project we were working on had been scheduled for completion in early October and the revised completion time was now set for early to mid-December. The fall market is a good time to sell since there are still multiple prospects. Competition equals a higher selling price and greater profits, but the same is not true for the winter months. In most cases, December to February is the least favorable time to be selling a home. Less competition equals a lower selling price, which equals less profit. So there I was feeling a bit vacant, as if my emotional database had gone to sleep.

At times like these, I ponder whether there might have been a sign that I missed, something the awareness revealed to me that might have been missed or misinterpreted. I left the situation in the hands of time by remaining silent within but stayed alert for a sign of feeling myself again. After a few more weeks passed and still no change—no brimming awareness, no feelings of peace or sorrow, still feeling as if I were floating in thin air—I decided to seek help. I went to see my friend Heather, an energy healer who works with chakras. She advised me that I might have stale energies inside my energy system. As we sat to talk, my feet in warm water and soft music in the background at a low hum, she questioned me on what was happening in my life.

I spoke and she listened with her eyes closed, as if deepening her connection with the cosmos. After a while, Heather advised that I was going through a transformation and that I should be patient since no one can put a time frame on these things, because they occur on universal time. She advised that there was nothing I needed to vacate in terms of habits or traits. "Just be patient," she said.

She also advised that not all my chakras were spinning, and after some more introspection on her part, she asked me to lie on her healing table with my eyes closed so she could realign my chakras. So I did. The background music was therapeutic and I quickly fell into stillness.

After a while, I felt as if my body became absent, for the only thing I could sense was my awareness. I could feel energy shifts around me at the same time. Whether they were Heather's or my own, I was not sure. I remained relaxed with complete trust.

At some point, the silence was broken. Heather advised that she was finished. I arose slowly from the lull, sat up on the edge of the table, and immediately recognized that something was very different. I took a few moments to absorb what I was sensing with my full and deep awareness.

Two things quickly became apparent. The first was I knew without looking in a mirror that a perpetual and radiant smile was chiseled into my face. Even though I was not trying or wanting to smile, I knew it was there. The second was the awareness and recognition that I was resonating in an energy sphere so high in voltage that it would disintegrate a human body. I just knew.

Heather had temporarily left the room, so I was able to just sit and feel and absorb. I was vibrating in pure energy, high-voltage energy, and I could feel my emotions and my thoughts on the outside of my being, as if my body had simply vanished. I could feel that the vibrations were moving beyond me, at a distance from where I stood, and when I moved, this massive energy moved too, always preceding me like a shadow when the sun is at your back. At this depth of vibration, I could see beyond the immediate now and knew the particulars of things that would happen beyond the present moment. This knowing was so profoundly clear it was as if the "yet to happen" events had already happened. Then suddenly the awareness came that I was enveloped completely in the full spectrum of pure spirit. This was a daunting fact to accept.

I sat motionless for some time with no thought and no emotions, just absorbing and being very still, very present. On accepting that I was immersed in this phenomenon, my first thought was to go out onto the street and walk amongst others to experience the dynamic movement of energies between this powerful spirit force that had encapsulated my whole being and the energies of others. I wanted to know how others would respond to this powerful light, and the vision came to me immediately of exactly what would happen. I would be able to see the light in others and it would be brimming with beauty at a level beyond the imagined, and I would be physically touching others and relaying to them how beautiful they are. I would be shedding love to them all as I looked upon and felt their God essence.

And the vision continued that some would feel a tranquil peace they had never felt before, and others would be perplexed but wanting to know more for feeling the radiance pulsating around me, and their being pulled into it. And still others would be wondering whether I was crazy, although their curious minds would feel the extraordinary pulse pulling their attention toward it.

I saw the whole experience while still sitting in Heather's healing room, as if it had already happened. Upon leaving her home, I had a second thought that perhaps I should go to the park instead, and again the internal knowing came rushing in that the animals would sense the energy and move toward it. I knew that I would feel the energy of the trees and plants and even the earth, and they too would feel the radiance around me. I knew the birds and squirrels would move toward the echo of the energy. I knew that if young children were close by, they too would move toward the invisible beam of celestial light.

Just before I reached my vehicle, I had a third thought. I wondered for a moment whether or not I would be able to drive my car while vibrating at this very high voltage, feeling as light as air, without a body. I was immersed in pure spirit, and wondered if spirit knew how to drive a car, and knew the directions to get me safely home. I received no prior knowing to that inquiry, so I approached the vehicle with trepidation, started the engine, and began to drive. I steered the car toward home. I wanted to maintain this experience for as long I could.

I reached home safely and remained inactive for the rest of the evening. I simply wallowed in spirit.

The vibration wore off around eleven o'clock that evening. I had lived and walked in the energy of pure spirit for approximately six hours. The interesting thing about this present moment, as I sit here writing this section of the book, is that while recalling the incident in mind, the vibrations came back. I am, in this very moment, feeling the steadiness of a high vibration both inside and outside my body, but to a much lesser degree. The memory replay reproduces the vibrant charges. I am reliving a past experience right here in this very moment.

Releasing Inner Child Wounds

Your Wounds Are Your Calling

Childhood Trauma

D id you ever consider the concept that all children become entrapped with various forms of childhood traumas predicated to them through naive parenting? Is that even possible? Are there any parents who know how to love their children so completely that no childhood wounds come about? Or is the truth that the psychology of life on this planet dictates that childhood is the time when traumas should develop, no matter how effective the parenting? Is that possible?

The answer is yes, and this is necessary for the damaged child to later become the student—and the student then to become the teacher/healer. It is the way of life on this planet that most people have unconsciously cultivated, due to their ignorance about how to live and love. It is due to lack of understanding of the innocence and fragility of the infant mind. Life in its perfection has adjusted itself to what humankind has done throughout the ages. Thus, children are born with rifts already in their energy bodies. But life and the system of energy that we are, have seen fit to communicate with us through our emotions to reveal the crux of our psychological damage, in order for healing to occur. Through healing, that is clearing the fractures in our mental and emotional bodies, we develop a better understanding of who we are. For those who are lucky enough to have realized that healing is required to find our true self, the payback becomes one of deeper spiritual awareness. This is necessary and fruitful, even though aspects of it seem like a game. The mechanics of life are perfect and we live that perfection through experiences and through who and what we become.

So what is the game? The game is that we all must grow up with some kind of trauma and these traumas come in a variety of forms and flavors. They hold within them the seeds for our unfolding into our purpose (our reasons for being here), which is the acknowledgment of our inherent gifts. The formulation for life, one could say, is victim to awareness to healer to broader conscious awareness. All these traumas carry the blueprint for what the child will become as a mature being—man or woman. These traumas carry specific habits within the psyche of man and these habits form the personality and mentality we beget during the critical years of growing and learning. They form the things we believe, the way we act, who we become, and the mental baggage we hold, which in turn creates more havoc in our life. And this remains so until we realize we need to do something about it to dissipate the troubles of the life we are leading. When we consciously begin to search for the justice to regulate our lives, a teacher or healer appears—someone with a higher vibration, with a mature gift that can aid us in the release of our baggage. This release brings us to an awareness of the system of energy that we are. If our courage to learn more is sound, we will begin to understand our sophisticated energy system to know how to manage our energies and our emotions through our bodies to avoid further blockages. This learning will heighten our awareness and bring us to the truth of who we are. We have lived under the influence of perception all this time and now are on a journey of deeper discovery into us. Our understanding will include the discovery and release of any barriers to our natural progression. We have placed our self on a path of being released from the bondage of human consciousness.

You are firmly on a path to a higher self. Know that the traumas you suffered in your early childhood and adolescence had within them the seeds for your new birth. The person into whom you will be molded through your healing, cleansing, and heightened awareness will begin to take form. A new beginning will present itself as you evolve into deeper awareness. You are beginning to understand yourself and life, and your purpose for enduring the traumas and for being here on earth will be revealed to you.

The Wounds Are Our Calling

For some, childhood woes can be devastating, such as unconscionable physical abuse, sexual abuse, or abandonment. But for most, the woes are less harsh and may include repeated put-downs causing the child to feel worthless and ineffectual. They may have come in the form of attacks on their usefulness, causing feelings of inferiority, or feelings of being ignored. This is the absence of support, which may lead to feelings of abandonment and self-hate.

Whatever your trauma, it houses you in an arena of lack. You are missing something and that thing cannot be a part of your store, for you know not what it looks like. When, for example, there is an absence of love during your childhood, one will grow through one's adolescent years and into adulthood not recognizing love, neither for it's giving nor it's receiving. But where there is an absence of something, there exists the seed for its attainment. For instance, a child who was deftly shy during her early developmental years and through her teenage years becomes an ardent speaker with complete comfort and finesse speaking in front of multitudes of people. Where did the courage come from? It came from the healing, because the healing removed the baggage and endowed her with awareness, leading her to her unique gift and purpose that allow her to exercise her brilliance through the blissfulness of spirit.

Let's examine the design for life, the blueprint for your evolution on planet earth. It is a design created in perfect harmony with the movement of life on the planet. Consciousness, in its perfection, has seen fit to allow everyone the same opportunities for self-realization, for being lifted out of the bondage of karma and human ignorance, and for evolving to higher states of being.

Let's have a look at the process of life.

- The inner child is damaged during the formidable years when the conscious mind is unaware and the subconscious mind is poised and ready for ardent emotional suggestions.
- During childhood, adolescence, and the early adult stages, the resident subconscious constructs cause instability and restlessness.
- Into adulthood, the desire for stability becomes paramount, and healers are sought.
- Getting help from healers reveals an awareness of the injuries and the consequential traumas.
- The incumbent becomes aware of their body, mind, subconscious, and energy system. Their knowledge and awareness of how their system works takes form.
- Removing wounds and blockages by themselves or by qualified healers, the incumbent's awareness increases. They are now the student.
- The incumbent is now able, through self-reflection and awareness, to process other inner childhood issues and blockages and their awareness increases even more. The student is maturing.
- A deeper inward search ensues through meditation and self-reflection. They now realize the deeper complexities of the body/mind/soul working together and a new direction is formed to move toward truth, toward wholeness, and toward knowing the self. The practice of spirituality becomes their primary pursuit.
- They are now on a path of continuous cleansing; encompassing deeper meditation, becoming seekers of knowledge and truth; cultivating deeper awareness; and becoming focused on aligning with their highest self in pursuit of exercising their divine gifts.
- The release of more wounds, deeper cleansing, and deeper understanding of the self, cause a radical inward shift in consciousness. Their awareness has expanded and the student is now the teacher/healer delivering goodness, love, care, oneness, harmony, and truth to others.
- Through deeper awareness, love becomes a stable foundation and their goodness becomes saintly. The teacher has matured into her divine essence.

The point to this is that wounds lead to a search for help, to recognition of how the body works, to knowledge of who we truly are and how life works, and to arriving at our purpose and our true self. This is the blueprint for the natural evolution of life on earth, and we are the pawns.

The dynamics of our being then revolves around our complete understanding of the traumas we suffered, through our endurance of them, through our living in the wake of their distortion upon our psyche, and through the havoc they formed within our character, distancing us from our true self. Now we are able to completely understand someone else's brand of the same or similar woe. Now we can heal and teach, and to the degree to which we are consciously aware, we will take charge in pursuit of truth and deliver our gifts, our birthright to humanity.

It is no wonder why most of us fall almost unconsciously into spirituality around the age of forty and beyond. This is typically when the kids are leaving home and now the parents are feeling that there has got to be more to life than what they have experienced thus far. When they are lucky, that search brings them to an inward looking, where the truth of who they are has always been, and the real journey of healing past wounds, releasing baggage, and getting to the nature of their true self becomes their full aim.

But let's look at this from a different perspective. What would life be, how would humankind benefit, and what of a united feeling of oneness throughout this earth if we started the healing and evolutionary process at an early age? Think about it. Instead of people being educated just academically with the only intent on earning a living, what would life be if we were also educated on the truth of who we are, such that we come to know our self and our individual destiny as well as the destiny of humanity? What of being educated on human values, such as fostering truth and the abilities to conduct ourselves rightly? What of fostering peace, love, and harmony and being prepared to service humanity instead of simply glorifying our own ego with scholastic certifications? Or thinking about how to love one's self, such that one can express love toward others? What would life be if we were taught early in our lives about the coming together of minds to solve differences of opinion and barter fairness instead of anger or violence? Our bodies are machines in which every limb, organ, brain cell, and all else work together for our movements and share in our joys and in our pains. Why then are we not being educated to work seamlessly together as one? And what of knowing and accepting a posturing of being virtuous at all times? Of becoming aware that we are one organism and that what is done to one is done to all?

The psychology of this planet dictates that we find ourselves, who we want to be, and what we want to do to earn a living during our teenage years. We must then solidify those pursuits through higher education during our late teens to early twenties. But how would life on earth shift if during that spectrum of time we became consciously aware and knowledgeable about life, about our singular self, and about our unitary self? This would create more spiritually evolved beings on planet earth. There would be no more wars, no more hate, and no disharmony. Oneness would become commonplace. Can you imagine?

Fracture

A child comes into this world with purity and bliss. They come being wholly dependent on their parents to be nourished in love and attention, which provides a feeling of safety and protection. They come with their hearts wide open to receive all that is good and sustainable to create, to abide in, and to hold beautiful memories from which to grow and experience life. They come to harmonize with life and deliver the fruits of their being. They are pure in their innocence and in their natural instinct to trust. But at very early stages in their development, their tiny little hearts are broken with abuse, trickery, and deceit. They become fractured. In an attempt to protect themselves, their subconscious minds create mental abstracts for present-moment protection. They are now broken, their innocence is gone, and they become willful. The subconscious mind holds these mental abstracts as triggers, and these abstracts become the bondages that will bind the child to certain reckless and destructive character traits and behaviors for decades to come.

The subconscious stores the mental patterns to protect the child from feeling the emotional shock or trauma again. And later on, it protects the young adult through triggers. A trigger is a subtle reminder in the form of a sharp emotional tug or strain to the heart. This occurs to prevent the young adult from stepping into a situation that will deliver the same or similar emotional shock or trauma. The paradox then takes form, for by protecting the child or young adult from these mental constructs, they develop unconscious negative personality inferences around the "protected emotional traumas," culminating into vacant characteristics or habits that they will unknowingly adapt. And these habits will follow them into their adult life. This binds their personalities and character into degrees of lack, causing mental confusion and psychological chaos. The child/adolescent becomes the unsuspecting adult who grapples with shame, guilt, rage, dishonor, and a loss of anything pure, and have no idea why this chaos is their state of being. This creates deep scars within the psyche, causing the adult to run fruitlessly on autopilot, being directed by these rogue psychological wounds of which they are not aware. Over long periods, these rogue wounds could mature into permanency; affix themselves as part of who we are at the level of our DNA. In this way, these wounds cause us a life of unconscious misery, blocking any fruitful internal growth. We cannot gain freedom with a subconscious stained with poisonous unconscious bondage.

Now we have found spirituality and want to become free. Unfortunately, the inner child stands at the doorway to our freedom and higher spiritual growth since, in essence, the inner child controls our life. This in itself is the awareness. You need the assistance of your inner child to remove the blockages so you can repair your fracture and move deeper into the light. The body and mind must be healed, leaving only health and harmony from within. The inner child must therefore, become healed, such that she can release the bondage she involuntarily accepted. She must be furnished with love and attention and feeling safe, to be able to erase the wounds. As the wounds are released, your vibration will expand. And your habits, behaviors, and emotional compass will be re-scripted to create a healthier mental attitude.

Healing the Inner Child

You must go back to the beginning. Children come to us in the light of Christ consciousness. They are pure and innocent, knowing only love. This is the essence of the inner child. It is your saving grace to step into the Christ consciousness, for you must restore the innocence. You must return to your purity by healing the inner child and releasing the bondage that has troubled your life for decades.

The self you have become, prior to merging with your inner child, is akin to a bird with a broken wing. It wants to soar through the air effortlessly and free, since that is its natural state. But with a broken wing, it cannot get off the ground. It is in an unnatural state. You must repair the inner child absolutely, and that will repair your broken wing. Then you can return to your innocence, to your freedom, for now you can fly.

The journey that the inner child was forced to sustain was not created by consciousness. It was created by man, in how man has come to live and come to relate with life. Life has simply related back to man what man has put into life. Man has dragged this innocent child from purity into the degradedness of human rubbish and now we must repair this. We have created a system of living that scares us even on our reentry to this planet. And now that we are aware of the blessings of the inner child, we must do the right things, both to repair the damage and to learn how to take care of our new born and our young so as not to rob them of their innocence and light. And if we can do this, life will shift to accommodate the freshness.

We must become educated about who we truly are, by taking the sacred journey to the self. We must come to live from our true essence, removing ourselves from the chaos that humanity has blindly created. We must ourselves become the light. Only then will we be equipped to rear our children, allowing them to maintain their light and their innocence, allowing the gifts they bring for humanity to flourish. We will be creating a new world with enlightened beings, a world of innocence and brilliance, a world devoid of treachery and mayhem, and a world without wars, hate, or separateness. This is our plight and the time to begin the liberation of a new earth is now. This is the dawn of a new beginning, a new hope for humankind.

Healing Modalities

There are various modalities for healing the inner child. You can choose to use multiple modalities. Some are through hands-on healing, some are through awareness, and still others are through hypnosis. But in all cases, you will develop a deeper awareness of the partnering of body, mind, and soul.

Mode 1

Self-Reflection (This requires your awareness.)

Most people would say that the content of their subconscious is hidden from them, but this is not true. The subconscious works to advise you of the entire negative emotional content stored within it, through triggers. With every initiation of a thought toward something that is a psychological or emotional trigger for you, the subconscious allows you to feel the emotions of that trigger in the present moment. For example, if a boy sees a girl he likes and wishes to approach her, the feelings of "She is too good for me," "She would never like me," come upon his psyche, crippling his forward movement toward that girl. If you are aware, you will recognize this sudden emotional prodding as a trigger indicative of a belief you hold about yourself. In this case, the belief may be "I am not good enough." You would have just recognized one of your subconscious blockages, and now the research begins.

Secure a place of quiet and privacy, and start the process of recalling the memory relative to the trigger. Take a few deep breaths, and relax completely. When the mind is still, simply intend for the origin of that particular inference "I am not good enough" to come to the forefront, and wait. All your memories reside in your subconscious and you are in the process of a recall. The subconscious mind is intelligent. It knows in the now which memory you are after and will bring that memory to the forefront. When the memory comes, you will feel as if you have travelled back in time, back to the age where the fracture occurred. You will relive that moment again, for you will see yourself and receive the full impression of what caused that particular trauma. You will see and feel your tenderness and fragility at that age and the horror that was taking place in your heart and nervous system.

I recall my first time going back in time. As I mentioned previously, I had always thought that my conscious memory of my childhood started at age twelve. But on following the rhythm of memory going backward, being guided by my friend Josephine, a therapist and healer, I was brought to the age of five years old and saw myself as I was then: in a particularly traumatic experience of feeling left out, being left alone, ignored. Josephine advised me that that particularly traumatic experience was the cause of my having what's termed "mommy issues."

In my life, the fallout of my "mommy issues" showed up in my long-term relationships with women. I needed to be the center of their attention, and to ensure I received that degree of attention, I made the relationship my priority and expected them to also make the relationship their priority without exception. Anything my counterparts did that did not resemble their putting the relationship above all else would bring trouble in the form of resentments. I held them to their word. A promise from them had to come through or else there would be ill feelings. I did not like to be kept waiting, not by anyone.

So here I was, merged with my five-year-old self, and I was feeling everything, in the here and now, that he was feeling in his present circumstance. We were one, for in that moment, I was him again, except I was also watching and feeling him through my adult eyes and emotions. In essence, I was in two places at once, sharing the same experience. The present awareness was that I felt and knew everything that was going through his mind and his heart. I felt the scars as if they were happening in the present moment.

Since then, I have gone back in time and spent much time with my five-year-old self. We frolic at the water's edge and love to run as fast as we can in the white sands. I told him that I am sorry for everything he is enduring and that he (which is me now) will grow up to be strong, resourceful, and successful at whatever he does. I informed him that he would become a man who is respected and admired. We hold hands as we stroll, and we always hug wholeheartedly before I leave. I watch him run back to his mommy and lie on her lap as she reads her books. I still cherish the memory of those moments with my inner child.

At some point after the revelation of the origin of my mommy issues, I was in my car and had a thought of going to see my mother to ask if she remembered the incident and time frame. I wondered if perhaps I could get an apology from her. I was listening to music in my car as I drove. Music keeps me grounded and in the flow with consciousness. Moments after I pondered that thought, something happened.

Suddenly a vivid energy flowed, like the feeling of rain running over my head and down through my body. It moved quickly, filling every cell and molecule inside me with light, and opening me up to the wisdom and the nature of its arrival. Its message was precise, with very broad content, which was now a part of me. It was a subtle remembrance filtered through me, the gist of which was: "all souls are contracted to other souls to deliver what is necessary for the evolution of all. Therefore, there is no need for an apology from my mother". I pulled over on the side of the road to allow the resonance, the vibrations going through my body, to subside. I dared not move in case something else might come. It must have been ten minutes before the vibrations subsided. The understanding was very clear. I turned the car around and headed home. I never mentioned any of it to my mother, for I was completely at peace with myself.

Don't be frightened to look at the horror your inner child has faced. Allow yourself to see what or who you were and what happened that caused these feelings inside you. Relive the emotion. See yourself and feel what you felt, and allow the feelings to move through you. Do not become engaged in the feelings, just observe. Watch and feel as if it were a movie. Feel it until it has run its course. You have just shone the light of consciousness on that emotional baggage; it is done, and now you must heal your inner child.

Go back in time. See your inner child at the age you were when that incident happened. Call her to you. Express your love for her. Hug her and let her know that you love her and that you are now aware of the burdens she carries. Tell her that she can now release that particular burden and that you will always be there for her. Say it with sincerity and do visit her often to remove other traumas as they arise, but always with the utmost love and gratitude.

You don't need to use the words above. Be in the flow with yourself and your truth. The words will come through intuition, so remain in the flow and be guided by your higher self. Just feel and impart whatever comes. Allow your empathy for him or her to flourish with heart truth. Just allow and you will be guided. Do it often, and ensure that you express absolute love and gratefulness to your inner child. You didn't have anyone to guide you at that age, but your inner child has you. Be good, be love, and it is done.

It is vital that you become "the witness," for your subconscious is always relaying to you your unconscious beliefs and habits through your feelings of lack or fears. These are the triggers for which you must become aware. Through your awareness, you can finally take the journey inside to rid yourself of them. These energies are dark energies that have become your blockages. They are your mental and psychological disharmony. Search vehemently for them. It is your duty to you.

Mode 2

Inner Child Meditation

(This meditation was developed by Dr. Hew Len and has been modified slightly for this book.)

You do not need to use the exact words presented here, but take time to reflect on how to speak to the inner child with love and understanding.

Your own words will come naturally as you feel the love and pain for your inner child.

The most important relationship in creation
is between mother and child.

Mother is the conscious mind with the choice to care or not. Child is the subconscious mind and carries all the memories and the burden.

Inner Child Meditation

Become still and take some deep breaths to still the mind.

- Breathe in slowly for seven counts. Hold for seven counts. Breathe out slowly for seven counts. Do this seven times.
- See the child and move toward the child slowly, as if she is a delicate flower.
- Let the child know that you are acknowledging her—you are aware of her. (In your own self, become aware of this being inside you.)
- With love in your heart, call the child to you. Allow her to move to you on her own terms.
- Tell her you are aware that she is a part of you; tell her you love her sincerely.
- Acknowledge all the hurts and pains that are in this child.
- Tell her you are sorry for what she is going through. Ask for her forgiveness for all the accumulated memories that you have accrued as sorrow and grieving pain.
- Always ask the child for permission to touch her or hold her.
- Go ahead and hold her. Show her love in your own way, using words and a loving touch. Let her know you are sorry for taking so long to come to her. Let her know you will visit her often.
- Ask over and over for her forgiveness for all her accumulated woes. Share exactly what you feel about what she is going through.
- You can mention specific traumas she has had to endure in this particular period of her life.

- Ask her to help you get rid of all this baggage and pain. Now offer the problems to the divine through the superconscious mind. Ask that the issues become set free.
- Give her more of your sincere appreciation and love, using words and gentle touching and hugs if she so wishes.
- Take another inventory of the issues you are releasing. For example, "Let us let go of the memories of being ignored."
- Say good-bye with deep appreciation and genuine loving affection. Win her over and allow her to intuit into herself.
- Now say good-bye.
- Breathe in slowly for seven counts. Hold for seven counts. Breathe out slowly for seven counts. Do this seven times.

Don't forget to visit your inner child regularly.

Other Healing Modalities

Inner Child Retrieval

This program goes to the heart of the wound to undo the negative patterns in your thinking, in your body, and in your spirit as well. This program works with your thoughts, beliefs, feelings, and nervous system. It's not enough to understand what happened and try to change your thinking. You also need to reset your nervous system, get rid of emotional flashbacks, and heal the body. This combination is the fastest and most effective way to real and lasting healing. This will increase your personal power, your creativity, and your joy.

Soul Retrieval and Inner Child Awakening Hypnosis

One of the coping mechanisms children use during their traumatic experiences is to leave the body just before the abuse takes place. This is why abused people often feel as if they are watching the abuse from outside themselves. This psychological removal causes the soul to become fragmented. The more traumas the child endures, the more the soul fragments. This is the reason so many adults who have suffered child abuse become disassociated and withdrawn, unable to get in touch with their feelings, and thus appear cold and detached.

Soul retrieval has been practiced by shamans for many centuries. The process reinstates the lost parts of the soul from this lifetime and from previous lifetimes. In this therapy, the client learns to accept the past and move past it by learning total forgiveness of self and others. The process combines inner child work with soul retrieval, which restores the soul. In hypnosis, the client is able to speak with their inner child. They are able to reassure the traumatized inner child that they, the adult, will not allow any further abuse to the child. They learn to speak to the abuser on the child's behalf. This cathartic process releases the anger that they both feel toward the abuser. Ultimately, they learn to forgive their assailant so that the inner child begins to feel that it is safe to return to their adult counterpart and become whole again. Sometimes the inner child needs further reassurance, especially if they are not convinced that the adult is ready and in the right mental state to hold their promise. The adult needs to continue to encourage their inner child until they feel secure and know that it is safe for them to return.

Reiki

Some elements of Reiki healing are based on the Asian tradition of medicine that is chi balancing, which over time has given rise to acupuncture, qigong, tai chi, and similar practices. These disciplines of treatment balance the radiant energies that regulate our body and our lives and cure physical, emotional, and psychological ailments. It is balancing the yin and yang within us, which out of alignment will cause discomfort, blockages, and restrictions in the body, leading to all ailments we refer to when we seek medical help or healing help.

Reiki is a natural system of energy healing. It is done by placing the hands on or near the recipient and moving energy over a series of locations on the recipient's body. This energy is our life force. It is the energy the Asians call chi, the universal force that permeates and sustains all living beings. It can be guided to heal through the hands and intention of the practitioner.

Practitioners can also work remotely. In this way, the practitioner runs Reiki energy through the affected parts of the body while visualizing their hands over specific body parts. Reiki is considered the "laying on of hands" or "spiritual healing" and is metaphysical in nature. It is one of the primary modes for inner child healing.

Parents, Be Aware

Children come to us with new information relevant for the evolution and perpetuation of life on the planet. This is necessary for humankind. Pay attention to them individually, their desires, likes, and direction, for they bring new perspectives and freshness to humanity. They come with the coding for improvements to create a higher life. They come to facilitate balance to the movement of life. They need absolute love and acceptance. Give it to them. Do not, however, attempt to bend them to your ways, for they are souls here to walk their own path and give to life what they bring. They are also here to create and experience life in and for their own divine purpose. Teach them well and assist them in *their* direction. They come here with their personalities already encoded in their psyche and the mark of who they are to become; what they will leave on the planet has already been predestined. They are unique, and that is purposeful, as no two humans have the exact same encoding for affecting humanity in the same way. Their uniqueness is theirs to live and thrive and become. Be very wary of attempting to shift their personalities to suit yours. They are sent from God to do their exacting part, as were you.

Clearing the Path to the Soul

Breath is one's only prayer, consciousness one's only god.
—Babaji

The soul is immortal. It cannot be destroyed or touched by man in any form.

The immortal soul, the eternal, through multitudes of lifetimes, has become identified with the physical bodies in which it has been clothed. Soul has become identified with the mind, the senses, and the intellect, and through such identifications, soul has become immersed in the ignorance and darkness that is planet earth's bequest.

Free Yourself

You are a divine being, for you are soul. But how you identify yourself makes a vast difference between becoming enlightened and remaining fragmented. If you identify yourself as the body, you can never be enlightened. If you identify yourself as soul, you are postured for enlightenment. Why postured? Can you see your divine self? Do you feel the eminence of soul within you? Or are you still in the illusion of separation from God and from all that there is?

If you cannot see or feel your soul, it is because your mind is festered in mud. You cannot see through the denseness of the mind and are living purely from mind. You must clear the muck from the mind to be able to see your true self and come to live and express who you are divinely. You must clear the bedlam of thoughts, ignorance, and misery from mind through discipline.

That discipline is through the practice of yoga. Yoga requires a physical, emotional, and mental commitment.

Realize that your soul is a temple of God, and through the repeated and proper practice of kriya yoga, your personality, your ego, your physical body, and all its metaphysical components will become a divine temple. The result is a fully enlightened soul, radiating divine love, light, and bliss through its physical incarnation, and into its surroundings, its relationships, and everything it does. This makes possible the spiritual progress of other souls, for the enlightened soul leaves peace and love in its path.

Yoga helps you to awaken from the illusion of God separation and helps you become aware of your angelic self, your true being that is of love and divine light—a true child of God. You will naturally feel, think, and act accordingly. Freedom and divine love becomes you. Yoga easily eradicates the fog of mind, allowing mind to evolve, then the soul can be easily seen. Soul becomes your beacon. Then you will be able to see and express the mystic of the soul through the things you do and whom you become.

What Is Kriya?

Man lives in the misery created by the recklessness of his own thoughts, attitudes, and judgments, none of which he can control. Kriya yoga teaches you to still the ripples of thoughts in the mind's lake through breath. It is considered the fast path to consciousness, speeding up the process of your evolution. Kriya is a process of spinal breathing, and the results are fast, effective, and certain. It eradicates the prospects of helplessness, unwillingness, and negativity, and it will remove all diseases and decay. As you breathe, you refine your body and your emotions, relieving the agony of emotional suffering. The cells in your body become and remain in a spiritually magnetized condition as the divine river of light flows through you.

What Is Kundalini?

Kundalini is experienced as a live electrical current moving rapidly through the spinal column. It is the primal energy of the universe that holds the universal design in place and creates all animate and inanimate forms. It is known as the serpentine power—the spark of life. It is the energy that animates the human body and governs the bodily functions through the nervous system. The movement of kundalini up the spine removes karma, negative mind stuff, and energy blockages, literally cleaning your system of all baggage and wounds and negativity. It effectively rewrites your DNA, giving you a new beginning, a new mind, and opening you up to deeper levels of awareness and emotions, while slowing the aging process. You have been thoroughly repaired and have been set on the path of a new beginning.

Kriya Kundalini Yoga

Yoga is the alchemy of change for the evolution of humankind. It is the science of the evolution of human consciousness. It builds in us the capacity to create a merging of body, mind, and soul to deepen our experiences in consciousness. It reveals to us how to see and relate to our self, how to treat others, and how to function effectively in the world. Yoga is transformative, moving the mind to a state of thoughtless awareness. It eliminates the constant sprouting of useless thoughts and brings ease and order. It removes from mind thoughts and obsessive images of depression, sorrow, or disease, all of which are identified with karma. Yoga unveils the vast ocean of awareness that lives behind your restless and copious thoughts, and opens the door to expose your divine nature, which is existence, consciousness, and bliss.

Yoga is a science of the self. It is a simple process of spinal breathing, but the results are immense and lasting. It severs the torment of lack and of emotional bondage, alleviating all disease and decay. Simply breathe, and as you breathe, your body, mind, and emotions are refined and purified. The anguish of emotional suffering ripples away with the effects of the practice and the results are profound. Yoga helps you to do what you are doing, but refined with brilliance. When this celestial river of light flows through you, it causes the cells in your body to become spiritually charged. This, in turn, allows mutations and ill growths, including cancer, to stop. Shake off, therefore, any laziness and practice regularly. Kriya yoga is the swiftest and simplest pathway to your divine self. During practice, allow whatever happens in your body to occur. Give in to the energies surging through you and become easy with the practice. You will learn how to let go and to stay in the flow.

Yoga transforms your being to a state of absolute harmony. It aligns your thoughts with your actions so there is no discrepancy in your truth. Truth does not come to you through thought. Ultimate truth comes to you through no thought. In thought, you are one thing, yet in your actions, you are something else. This disharmony in you typically creates regret. The transformative agent of yoga uproots the animal drive from you and transforms you in thought and in deed. Now your thoughts and your deeds are aligned—no disparity and, therefore, no regrets. Your trained mind has gone deeper into your deeds to become a part of your being. This is the transformation of the breath. This is the dynamic shift you hoped and prayed for. This is the transformation of yoga. Breath then becomes your prayer, your petition.

My first experience with kundalini yoga was at a studio in downtown Toronto where people practice various disciplines of kriya yoga. I took the subway to the studio since it was in a heavily trafficked area of the city. I had not been on the subway for twenty-five years so I felt a little strange, almost out of place. I mentioned to the teacher that I had not done this before. She said not to worry but just to follow her lead.

There were only three of us in this class at that time. The practice began and I had no problem following the lead. I could tell the others were also new at this. We were constantly looking at each other to ensure we stayed in the correct posturing and movements and in the right keys while sounding.

Approximately half an hour into the routine, something started to happen inside my body. My spine began to convulse, and as I continued to follow the rhythm, the convulsion became deeper and more vigorous. The inside of my spinal column was moving wildly on its own. I had no control. I felt a little afraid, not knowing what this was and what to expect, so I quietly mentioned to the teacher that there was irregular movements in my body for which I have no control. I was surprised with her response. Quite calmly she said, "Good. Just be with it." So I relaxed the mind, but inside my spinal column, I felt as if a war was raging.

I felt very odd not having any control over my own body. I wondered if the kundalini energy was rising in me and if this meant I might become enlightened in the here and now. That was a bit frightening too. I wondered if I was ready for the responsibilities of enlightenment.

When the practice ended, the convulsion was still moving in me so I sat there motionless, my eyes still closed, in a state of allowing. Perhaps twenty minutes passed before the convulsing calmed.

I opened my eyes and realized that the other two students were also sitting motionless. But now, with my eyes open, I could sense more appropriately. I felt as if I had been washed from the inside. I felt like an empty vessel. I felt a bit like a bulb, as if radiant light was shining from within me. I was feeling all these peculiar feelings. I wanted to ask questions about what was happening, but something inside me also wanted to keep the silence and just continue to feel the experience. I sat there with eyes closed, just feeling and being.

When I stood up from my seated position, many things were different. There was a feeling of lightness, as if I could float if I desired. I walked to the closet to fetch my street clothes, but I don't remember feeling the floor beneath my feet. Even while changing my clothes, I felt as if my feet were not touching the ground. I actually thought that perhaps I would not be able to walk back to the subway and I should wait until this feeling subsided. I felt that the gentle wind outside might blow me over.

By the time I reached the street, I realized my walking and uprightness was steady and that these feelings of drunkenness I was experiencing were all on the inside of me. When I reached the subway, other feelings had emerged. Everyone I passed or noticed was radiating glowing beams of light. I could feel the bulb of energies around them. I could feel the insides of them. I could feel sadness and loneliness and all levels of feelings from all those who came into my field of vision. I knew exactly what was going on emotionally in everyone. I felt it all.

So the journey back home on the subway was very different. I was seeing and knowing everything, but not through my eyes nor my intellect. I was seeing inside others and knowing their pain or their joy. At some point, the awareness came that I was seeing through the mind of spirit, for everyone was strikingly radiant in his or her own way. There was a very deep calm on the ride home. I felt pure peace, bliss. I became aware of a perpetual smile that was planted on my face the whole time, and these feelings followed me home.

I did not become engaged in anything after arriving home. I remained rested in that humble space of pure spirit that enveloped my being. Now I know how it feels to walk completely in spirit, for I existed completely in spirit for two hours while wearing a human body.

Breath and the Spine

The quality of the life you seek and the unearthing of the bliss you pray for rest in your spine. Breath is the practice of spiritual growth, and when you have developed breath control, breathing becomes subtler and subtler into life energy, as you develop life control. The spinal cord connects heaven and earth. It is your human connection to the cosmos, where spirit meets matter. The spinal column is the channel through which cosmic energy filters through the body to animate life into the body, to keep your heart beating, your organs functioning effortlessly, and your breath to remain constant. Breath is life. Breath dissolves the karma, which is latent in the pranic lotuses of the spine. You become awakened to higher dimensions and deeper awareness as your life is being renewed.

The spine is the axis of your being. Although the spine is not located in the center of your body, it represents the center of your being. Life, mind, emotions, and desires all flow from the spine. The physical and astral plains converge in the spine, at the centers of which are the chakras. The chakras accept the immense cosmic forces from the universe and regulate them to a degree that the body is able to filter and absorb. Through the presence of these physical and psychological energies inside the chakras, the creation of our thoughts, desires, and feelings are formed inside the body and mind. This is the means to motivate and move us toward progress in the world.

The physical spine is the body's structural support center for the body and mind. It is the nerve cells within the spinal cord that carry all the signals that are required to sustain our states of being, including our aliveness, awareness, our sleep, and our dream states. The spine is also the root of our individual consciousness. For most, their awareness is summoned from the five senses, which is severely limiting. But during yoga, one must take one's full awareness into the spine. One must visualize the eruption of this divine cosmic energy (prana), moving forcibly through the spinning lotuses and taking with it our negative thought forms and our karma. Then one must release one's emotional baggage and clear a path to a fresh new mind. This is the healing property of moving the breath, prana, through the spine. This is the rebalancing of the self. This is getting us in touch with the vast cosmic forces that are our bread and butter for transforming ourselves into beings of power and light. It allows us to move our levels of awareness to superior heights. Yoga postures and pranayama breath control create a strong and flexible spine, opening all channels and tributaries of the spine to support the flow of prana, nerve impulses, and mental and spiritual energies.

Let's take a closer look at the spinal column. The seven main chakras that reside from the base of the spine to the crown generate the patterns of the auric field. This is your aura, the magnetic field of light around your body that resonates your thoughts and feelings. Their interconnection comes from two currents: the physical body and the spiritual body. As these two centers intertwine as one around and through the chakras, they form an energy sphere, a bridge of infinite light, connecting the physical with the spiritual. This is all that we are: a brilliantly vibrant pathway from matter to spirit and from spirit to matter—one source. These spinning and shifting chakras take us on a journey through life: the spiritual living from existence and the physical living from experience—two as one.

The Sushumna is the main and most important channel that guides cosmic energy entering the human system through the length of the spine. It is the connection between the crown chakra, which is on the top of the head, and the root chakra at the base of the spine. It facilitates a hard connection with all chakras, bringing them into alignment. With controlled breaths, these seven spinning chakras become the nexus for our transformation in consciousness, the gateway to deeper awareness and experiences. And for the body, it heals all ailments, returning the body to its optimum state. The requirement of this transformation begins with the breath.

Nadis are smaller channels running alongside the Sushumna. The two main Nadis carry psychic current that sustain nerves and plexuses, as well as the subtle nerves of mind and of the feeling self or being. It should be noted that these gross nerves and plexuses (physical) have close relationship with the subtle nerves (astral). Vibrations that are produced in the physical centers (the body), such as during yoga or prescribed breathing practices, have the exacting desired effects in the astral (spirit) realm as well. These astral centers or plexuses exist in the spine, brain, and esoteric bodies and are our human connection to spirit, to planet earth (which is also a living sphere of energy), and to the universe.

These two principal Nadis are the Ida, which carries feminine energy that nourishes and purifies the body and mind, and the Pingala, carrying the masculine solar energy, which brings vitality, physical strength, and efficiency while purifying and cleansing the body. The two Nadis are activated by breaths from the left and right nostrils respectively and stimulate the left and right sides of the brain as well. The breath you take through your nostrils, therefore, stimulates the brain and flows through the main channels, connecting the astral centers of vital force called lotuses (chakras), starting at the crown chakra (heaven), ending at the sacral chakra (earth), and connecting all other chakras in between. These centers of concentrated energy radiate life-giving light. Once all lotuses begin to spin, the connection between heaven and earth has been made "as above, so below," causing powerful changes within the body and mind. What happens in the physical body also happens in the astral bodies. Yoga, therefore, creates a glorified merger of the individual consciousness with the universal consciousness—two becoming one.

The left and right nostrils are connected to the Ida and the Pingala respectively (the two Nadis running alongside the Sushumna), which are the main channel of the spine. A controlled breath awakens both the physical and astral agents of the spine, creating a vortex of energy of transformative proportion. Your breath, your awareness, and your mind are pointed with intent; they are fused into a potent force which creates a spinning vortex of energies that travel up and down the spine, purifying and transforming the body and mind and raising your level of awareness. Any impurities in the body are removed, allowing your natural state of being to resonate blissfully in the present moment.

The current, moving up and down the spine, induces other smaller channels running perpendicular to the main channels. These smaller channels, consisting of interconnecting streams of energy, converge with the spinal current and carry the currents between the spine and the outer edge of our subtle bodies into the astral plains, which is our aura. These channels act as a magnetic force that holds the aura and subtle body in place, such that our physical and nonphysical bodies function as one body. Be aware that "controlled breaths" stimulate healing in both the physical and in the astral plane simultaneously.

The Awakening

Breathing through the spinal cord transforms the latent impressions (mind stuff) stored in the subconscious into positive life energy. When the breath moves through the sushumna inside the spinal cord, it comes into contact with the astral plexus, the chakras, and when it passes through the chakras, it nullifies your negative karma along with bodily diseases, mental diseases of stress and tension, and emotional suffering. All is transformed to positive life energy. This process of moving the breath through the chakras must be done with a strong mind, with pointed concentration and intent.

Your DNA is held in the astral chakras, in the nonphysical. This is the vortex of energy linking the spiritual to the material. Your DNA inside the chakras records all your past deeds and actions through all of your lifetimes. You cannot hide from your past karmas; there is no escape. Kriya breath, while moving through the spinal cord, passes through the crevices in the spinal cord and erases the recording of your past karma from your DNA. In a friction-like manner, it burns your past karma from your DNA. This creates a new life awakening. This is what kriya yoga does. It is the dynamic process of the evolution of spiritual consciousness. The more concentrated your mental intent during the process, the more karma and negative mind stuff will be removed from your energy field..

The Rising Kundalini

It is believed in the yoga philosophy that the serpentine energy of the goddess Kundalini-Shakti lays coiled three and half times around the Muladahara, the base chakra, holding matter together as the creator of all being. Once we have seen our true path, via the third eye, the serpent becomes aroused, awakened, and starts her journey up the spine, awakening each chakra as she moves, and ending with the piercing of the crown chakra. She is seeking her divine partner Shiva who abides in pure spiritual awareness—two beings as one. They dance in energetic embrace, interconnecting the energy systems of physical body and the soul, and now her journey is complete. Sahasra, the seventh chakra, blossoms emanating from the dimensionless point of consciousness within—awake, aware, intelligent, and divine. There are no limits to the nature of consciousness. Shiva gives birth to stars and journeys you to the heart of the cosmos, to the realm of divine mind, the source of all. Each chakra bathes in the current of consciousness. We are that consciousness. We are "the rainbow bridge to the world."

When kundalini awakens in you, it optimizes all of your nervous systems and glands.

The heightened consciousness emanating from your soul can project itself with eminence into the world. It arouses a movement within you toward manifestation, taking the unseen and making it visible. This makes love an action that you easily and fervently actualize into the world, caressing the whispers of the soul and guiding its embrace into your words, such that what you say is your absolute truth, wrapped in gentleness and kindness, and equipped to write beauty and peace upon the heart of the ones to whom you are speaking. This is becoming wholly responsible for aligning the outcomes of your actions and deeds with your heightened awareness. You cannot escape the responsibility of your higher calling. Recognition of your identity and your awareness becomes commonplace, and you comprehend them both from a place of sacredness. Now the gap between your consciousness and yourself, who you truly are, has been significantly closed, for you are operating from that place of love, which is the true nature of "the self." This is a place from which compassion is initiated in the face of all polarities. You will walk the path of the heart, and uniquely, you deliver your brand of yourself into the world with little effort.

Your levels of awareness will multiply. The awakened kundalini creates delicate shifts in the subtle bodies within the meridians and chakras. You become aware and open to many more levels of awareness, including different emotions you may not have experienced before. You may experience subtle insights that you can neither explain nor express, even though you feel and are aware of their depths. Just imagine that deep breathing can cause such significant changes in you, altering your physiology and mind. It clears the path to enlightenment, thus returning you to the divine. Now you can take flight to higher dimensions and soar.

Yoga and Spiritual Progress

If you practice meditation, yoga, and controlled breathing, there is a constant updating of your spiritual progress. This includes an updating of your circumstances, and since your individual present is derived from your individual past, you will see significant changes that have become a part of your being—no fuss in trying, less effort in doing, and more of just "being." You will find yourself taking actions that are worthy and will create no regret. You will find that your meditation will amplify your thoughts and deeds that bring out joyous results. Any thoughts of illnesses, diseases, strife, or foul will slowly dissipate. Dwell on light and love and what you desire, for you are what you think. Use the tremendous energies of mind to penetrate and pierce the lotus shrines during yoga to get to the divine. Don't waste your powerful thought energies on useless mind stuff during the practice. Deliberately focus the energies during yoga and train the subconscious mind by repeating the same mantras every day. (Mantras can reduce or mitigate your karma.) Make this your daily ritual, your natural rhythm for conscious living and returning home to the divine.

Withdrawing Consciousness from the Senses

To amplify the results of kriya, a powerful technique is to withdraw the consciousness from the senses. When the mind is involved in thought, there are usually desires or other thought forms that arise. Kriya is one of the best ways of withdrawing the consciousness from the senses and into the spinal center. When both consciousness and prana are moved through the spinal cord, the power it engages is synonymous to recharging a battery using consciousness. Deeply rooted karma and mind stuff residing in the psychic centers in the chakras will be burned out by the concentrated movement of prana and mind through the centers.

These exercises will also stop the mind from being blind, from its habitual sanctity, from its outward only projection with no inward looking. It will become easier for you to sense more of what's happening in your body and with your body. You may even recognize for the first time that your saliva has a taste to it. You will relish the subtle experiences that come from the body. We should strive for an awakened mind; it does not need arms and legs and entire body. It will create an inner peace. Repeated practices are going beyond mind; this is how you train the mind, and mind at some point will start concentrating on the self. So take mind into the body. It can be trained. This will create new habits of mind through practice. Do kriya in the morning and at night.

Yoga and the Layers of Mind

What happens to the mind after kriya? First, random thought forms create little whirlpools on the surface of the mind's lake. These pools create continuous ripples obstructing newer, more productive thoughts. During kriya yoga, these whirlpools are stilled and lengthened by the elongated rhythmic breaths of kriya yoga. This removes all deeply embedded thought forms or visual images from the mind, both of which could have followed you through countless lifetimes being embedded in your subconscious. The surface of the mind's lake becomes still, ready to accept more productive thoughts and visual images. Second, meditation becomes deeper and more sustainable, since the mind is quiet, at ease, abiding in the present moment. The effects of deeper meditation will readily reveal themselves in your life. Third, kriya meditation takes you deeper into the mind of expanded consciousness and into the state of ecstasy. Keep practicing and you will behold your divine soul.

Your mind becomes etched with the willful thoughts that are most prevalent inside your mind space. These thoughts travel with you through many lifetimes, writing your karma along the way. You carry the baggage of all your karma with you; therefore, you carry specific karmic thought and thought forms that create the accessories of your prevalent attitude of mind. Mind associates with emotions, and emotions associate with the breath. Breath associates with the body and senses. This is the dance of going through worlds and lifetimes to learn right and wrong, learning the lessons of life and reacting to them accordingly as per free will. This creates many traumas or joys in the subconscious. When conscious mind and superconscious mind are clear of all these thoughts, then you realize that you are the immortal soul and not the corrupt body. When the body and mind are no longer disturbed, enlightenment has taken full course. Enlightenment means no further disturbances from the body or mind, and now you can take flight like the swan.

Life and the Breath

We are each born with a specific number of breaths to be taken before we pass from this place and return home. That number of breaths is the only thing that marks the length of your stay here on planet earth. Whether you leave earth via a car accident or from sudden infant death syndrome five minutes after you were born, your body reached its limit of breaths.

The average person takes 21,600 breaths in twenty-four hours, which equates to fifteen breaths per minute. One of the benefits of kriya breathing technique is that the breaths are lengthened, and if you persist in doing kriya breathing regularly, the natural rhythm of your breath elongates and lengthens to roughly 9,000 breaths per twenty-four hours, which are approximately six to seven breaths per minute. The remaining 11,000 breaths per twenty-four hours that you did not take are added to your life span. You are, therefore, increasing the longevity of your life. And at the eleventh hour, you go into samadhi. Samadhi is a state of intense concentration. In the realm of form, samadhi is a deep and intense focus on the present moment, without distraction or attachment but with a lingering awareness of oneself. When the "I" disappears, there is a complete falling away of body and mind, and the absence of reflection and recollection become present. There is no memory of experience, because the subject and the object are completely merged—a complete recognition of the existing non-separation from source. Samadhi loosens the grip of projected reality, showing us that the world we perceive isn't as real as we think it is. Samadhi opens the door to enlightenment. In Hindu yoga, this is regarded as the final stage at which union with the divine is reached (before or at death). You pass through the gates of death, but you remain conscious. Samadhi is conscious death or conscious sleep.

Man's only purpose here is to seek God. "Where is God?" you might ask. God is the essence you see or feel when you look at someone. God is in the loving embrace of your wife, husband, or your lover. God is in the kindness bestowed onto you by a stranger. God is within the deep desires of your heart. God is the glitter in your eyes as you look toward the moon at night. God is behind every good action or deed. Look a little closer. God is where you are. But we become deceived by minor things and forget stillness, peace, tranquility, and beauty, which is God.

God, divinity, and consciousness are the sole purpose of our journey.

8

Life Energy via Controlled Breath

A Vortex of Healing Energy

Breath Mastery is self-mastery. Pranayama is life energy generated by controlled breathing. Controlled breathing means being in control. Being in control begets vitality, calmness, quiet, and brings an aliveness of "being" permeating through you. Breath control begets self-control. Breath mastery begets self-mastery. Breathless is deathless. Change any negative mood by changing your breath. Breath is life; so insist on watching your breath during your daily activities. Breath should be calm, controlled, and peaceful. There is no life without breath.

—Guru Vandana Osho

The cosmic energies of pranayama moving through the physical and spiritual bodies wield incredible healing power. In May 2015, I was diagnosed with prostate cancer. As far back as 2012, I was told that I had an enlarged prostate. Through conversations with my urologist, it seems that once a prostate becomes enlarged, the medical professionals require frequent PSA tests. PSA tests, although not totally reliable, can help detect small tumors that do not cause symptoms. Over time, my PSA score went from 3.2 to 7.6, climbing slowly as time passed. During that time, I had two separate biopsies—very uncomfortable—and two MRI reports, to watch for the development of cancer in the prostate. Through these tests, it seemed there had been no reparation or healing of the prostate back to its normalcy. "Is there no cure to get the enlarged prostate back to normalcy?" I asked. His answer was no. "So I am just biding my time in wait for cancer to appear?" He didn't respond.

I found that very difficult to understand, since there are so many plants and roots on this planet that can heal any and all diseases. Some months earlier, I had included kapalbhati pranayama exercises into my daily regime. I had learned of the capabilities of this pranic force as it moves through the physical and spiritual bodies. The urologist scheduled a biopsy for me in July 2015. The biopsy was to assess the severity of the cancer and confirm the type of radiation or other procedure to be used to remove the cancer. I advised him to book my biopsy appointment for six months from this day, instead of three months. He said they wanted to catch the cancer early before it became worse. I insisted on waiting six months. He reluctantly complied.

Over the next six months, I practiced the kapalbhati pranayama exercises using the pranic breathing techniques. Through each exercise, I could feel the enormous energy surging through my body, my organs and my chakras. With a still mind, I focused the light of this pranic force into my prostate, into my bladder, into my kidneys, and then into all other organs. The higher mind knows when healing is taking effect, for I felt it in my being and knew that my prostate was being healed. I allowed this pranic force to move through all parts of my body, including my outer skin. I felt the power of prana and knew that there were shifts happening in and outside my body.

In November 2015, I went as scheduled for my biopsy. The result was there was no cancer. Since then, I completed another PSA test, and the score dropped from 7.6 to 5.2. The urologist was perplexed. He kept looking at the results, wondering if they were correct.

Pranayama

In Sanskrit, the word *pranayama* is composed of two parts: *prana* and *yama*. Prana is vital energy that manifests itself as the energizing force animating life into the body. It is cosmic in nature and carries the power of the entire universe, revealing itself as a living entity in us through the miracle of the breath. Yama means control and describes the action and movement of prana inside the body. When this force is moved through the human body with purpose and control, it is called pranayama. The sages define pranayama as regulation of incoming and outgoing breath coupled with retention and intention.

A comprehensive knowledge of prana and its function is absolutely necessary for adapting pranayama as part of your daily ritual. Here I will explore the universal force that is prana and your relation to it.

Prana is the spiritual life principle of the universe, and it is everywhere. It is the culmination of all energies that exist in the universe and, therefore, is the universal system, the principle and force of energy across time and space. It is the latent power manifested throughout all of nature's forces and movements and within and around man and beast and everything else that lives. It is the power that remains motionless during cosmic dissolutions, when planets, continents, or worlds are at rest to refresh and remold themselves with new changes of force, whether for geological redistribution of soil or water, for a change of climate, or for a shifting of the axis. Prana waits in a motionless state until the vibrations are right and then moves to bring forth new beginnings, new forms, to reestablish life and continuity. Prana is the life through which universes are born.

Whatever lives, moves, breathes, or has life is but an expression or manifestation of prana. Prana causes the eyes to see, the ears to hear, the skin to feel, the tongue to taste, and the nose smell. It is prana that causes the brain and the intellect to function as they do. It is prana that animates your being and your physicality so you delight in the melody of music; your skin vibrates from the words of a speaker; you indulge in gut-wrenching cries or languish in laughter from an incident that touched you deeply. Whatever you behold in this world, whatever moves, works, or has life, is but a manifestation of prana.

Prana is the breath that fills your lungs, which is life itself. It is prana that pumps the blood from the heart into the blood vessels and into the brain. Your bodily functions, such as digestion, excretion, and secretion, are through prana. The mind is then able to think and inquire into the nature of Brahman.

Antahkarana, a division of prana, is the totality of all minds and forms the entire psychological process, including our emotions. It is a unit that functions with all parts working together as one. It includes the following:

- manas, which is the thinking mind that controls will and resolution and is related to the five senses and cravings for new and pleasant sensations and emotions. It exists as the mental body;
- buddhi, which is the intellect or higher mind that controls reason and decision-making and holds wisdom, intuition, and experience. It is the witnessing mind;
- chitta, which controls memory and consciousness, including remembering and forgetting; and
- ahamkara, which is the ego that identifies the self, the body, as "I."

So what of prana? Prana is the link between the astral body and the physical body. When death takes place in the physical body, the slender link of prana connecting the astral body to the physical body is cut, withdrawing the prana into the astral body. Prana takes a higher place than mind or the senses and is present even when the mind is absent during sleep. Therefore, prana plays a more vital part than the mind. Prana is present and functioning from the moment a child is conceived, whereas the organs and senses begin to function only when their special abodes, such as the ear or nose, are formed. Through the vibrations of psychic prana, the mind is maintained and thoughts are produced. It is prana that allows you to see, hear, talk, sense, think, feel, know, and exercise your will. Prana is Brahman.

The seat of prana is the heart, and its function is respiration. Prana is responsible for excretion from the lower abdomen to the anus. It is responsible for digestion, swallowing, sleeping, awaking, the circulation of blood, eructation (belching), hiccupping, blinking, and opening the eyes. Prana induces hunger and thirst, yawning, decomposition of the body after death, and everything in between.

How Prana Is Expended

Prana is expended through the things you take for granted, such as your thinking, willing, doing, moving, talking, processing, writing, and all the rest that is life and living. A healthy, strong person has an abundance of prana, which looks and feels like vitality. Prana is supplied through solar energy from the cosmos but also by food, water, and air. The supply of prana is what nourishes the autonomic, central, and peripheral nervous system—the parts of the body that coordinate the voluntary and involuntary actions and transmit signals to and from parts of the body. Prana in the air is absorbed by breathing. The excess is stored in the brain and nerve center. When the seminal energy is sublimated or transformed, it supplies an abundance of prana to the system, which is stored in the brain in the form of spiritual energy.

The yogi stores a great deal of prana through the regular practice of pranayama, just as a battery stores electricity. That yogi radiates strength and vitality all around. He becomes a powerhouse, and those who come in close contact with him absorb prana and receive strength, vigor, vitality, and exhilaration of spirit. Just as water flows from one vessel to another, prana actually flows like a steady current from a developed yogi toward a weak person.

Prana is a force that touches everything. Anyone who stands broadly in his or her own authority, holding little or no fear inside, who exhibits charisma or power of personality, will possess abundant prana. Prana is what others feel when they are around you, whether the feeling is one of power and influence or one of frailty. A person who is successful in life, one who is more influential and more captivating or interesting than others, will have abundant prana. It is the power of your prana that others sense as strength or magnetism that draws them to you.

Benefits of Pranayama

The goal of pranayama is to significantly improve your overall health and the function of all the organs in the body. As you breathe, a vortex of healing energies is formed inside the body, not unlike the spinning vortex at the center of a hurricane. This wheedling energy force moves through the body and heals everything that is not in alignment with the perfect resonance of the body. Whether your ailment is mental, emotional, or physical, none of it can withstand the power of this universal pranic-healing force. The yogis say, "Let the defects be burned up by pranayama."

Physical

The student will become free from all sorts of diseases, for pranayama...

- removes the impurities of the body, the senses, and the mind;
- reduces the heart rate as well as the wear and tear of the heart;
- helps the body get rid of excessive fat and weight;
- enhances the functioning of several organs, including kidneys, pancreas, intestines, diaphragm, lungs, and heart;
- removes toxins from within the body;
- prevents various diseases by strengthening the immune system;
- enhances the circulation of blood throughout the body; and
- reduces blood pressure by relaxing the body and soothing the nerves.

Mind

The mind becomes fit for concentration by removing the veil of disturbing energy obstructing the light of consciousness. The mind further becomes stable and steady like a flame in a windless place. Through pranayama, your natural breathing will be lessened, which will make it easy to stop the breath. Thus the velocity of the mind will be slowly lessened by making it stable and focused for higher concentration and deeper practices. Absent-mindedness and distraction are removed. Lack of drive and laziness disappear, and the mind becomes focused and purposeful, transcending ordinary experience.

For now, mind exists in the superconscious plain higher than that of reason, moving beyond the limit of concentration. In this state, knowledge simply comes without any mental wrestling. This is achieved through manipulation of the subtle forces of the body to cause them to give an upward push into the higher regions of mind. When the mind is this raised, it begins to experience higher facts and higher knowledge. Such is the ultimate object of pranayama. The control of the vibration of prana means the student becomes in touch with the fire of supreme knowledge and deeper realization of the self. Pranayama increases the quantum of this life force (prana) so that it can reach out to the "hidden" recesses of the brain. This helps in expanding the human faculties and retarding degeneration.

Discipline

Pranayama develops the lungs and those who practice it will possess a melodious voice. The body becomes lean, strong, and healthy, and one's appetite becomes keen. The digestive fire is amplified, the face becomes luminous, the eyes sparkle, and one becomes radiant. Negative emotions, such as depression, anger, arrogance, and greed, simply disappear. Steady practice arouses inner spiritual light and peace of mind.

Pranayama is the magic wand for attaining perfection in all spheres of life.

Pranayama also paves the way for effective meditation. Meditation is the practice of stilling the body and mind, such that what you concentrate on becomes an energetic force onto itself. Pranayama also has been referred to as the art of effective breathing. You cannot practice pranayama efficiently without disciplined, pinpointed attention on the breath, drawing your complete awareness into the breath. This favorably trains the mind to become still, focused, and purposeful. This is meditation. Your mind assists you in becoming more aware of your breath, drawing you into the activities of the breath, which prepares you for the stillness of meditation.

Prana and Karma

Prana purifies your consciousness, releases your reckless mind, and allows the light of knowledge to shine through. Your karmas are attenuated, and with zealous practice, they are eventually destroyed and the pure self is revealed. Just as fire destroys the fuel, pranayama destroys your collections of sin. The benefits of pranayama are, therefore, physical, emotional, and spiritual.

There are many techniques for moving the pranayama breath through your body, each with its own significance for healing. Typically in any posturing for pranayama, several techniques will be involved, one after the other, with a one-minute or two-minute break between techniques. This is so the effects of the technique can take form inside your body and you will actually feel the movement of this universal energy surging through your spinal column. Here, I will speak on just one technique.

Kapalbhati

Kapal means "head." *Bhati* means "purification." This particular movement of prana purifies your head, and when purified, you become a different person. It is a very forceful inhalation and exhalation process. It brings a significant amount of oxygen into the system, and when you exhale forcefully, it removes toxins by burning them like fire. In fact, the Western name for this particular technique is "breath of fire."

This technique brings absolute transformation. It is a type of pranayama and pranic force that we need in our lives. The process brings more oxygen into the system, into the brain, lungs, and blood, and takes carbon dioxide out of the system. This is building your system the right way. The techniques of breathing are very specific; therefore, the breath must be done correctly, for herein lies a myriad of benefits. The physical benefits are that you become totally relaxed in mind and body. Any sickness or ailments in the body will be removed with consistent practice. It lowers your blood pressure, and it removes stress from the body and brain. The more oxygen that filters through the brain, the more stress is released. The energy frequency, or your spiritual vibration, will increase from this full body detox, the primary benefit from which is that your energy frequency moves higher, moving you out of the lower frequencies that are synonymous with becoming depressed. This optimum state is the nexus for your spiritual, mental, and physical growth. Your restless mind dissipates and you become calm and steady. Your ability to concentrate improves vastly, allowing you to go deeper into meditation. Your awareness improves significantly, such that you come to see and understand more of yourself.

> Everything that was, is, or shall be, is nothing but the different
> modes of expression of the universal force called prana.
> —Paramhansa Yogananda

The practice of pranayama has become a part of my daily ritual. It is the first thing I do after sliding out of bed every morning. It brings immense stillness into my sphere. When my mind is at rest, there is a steady peace that pervades me from the inside. There is no noise going on in the background, for conscious mind is also at rest. The prevalent feeling is one of silence, always watching and being informed, and feeling inspired. Life feels without strain, unencumbered, easy, and free. I don't really need to sit and meditate as much anymore, for as I move about my day, the observer is always keen, always watching and revealing things to me. I am still surprised at what comes up sometimes: parts of my past baggage that I thought had been released have not completely gone. Fragments remain, but what I find fascinating is the dichotomy among the conscious mind (the inquisitive child), the subconscious mind (the driver/director), and consciousness (the observer). They interplay completely, without direct communication with each other. For instance, when I am driving my car and come to a stop at a traffic light, conscious mind would be looking all over, watching people and wanting to see what's going on, being inquisitive. When the car begins to move, conscious mind would be wondering why the car is moving since the light is red. But when conscious mind glances forward, it notices that the light is green and that the car, being driven by the subconscious (the driver) is already halfway through the intersection.

The subconscious does not need the eyes of the conscious mind, for it is the driver of our lives and has no time to look elsewhere other than where it is going. Consciousness is sitting back and watching all this and it is consciousness that lets me know, through awareness, that the conscious mind was not fully present in the moment, for it is again looking out the side windows. I gathered from this orchestration that the crux of our evolution is this: when conscious mind begins to look at what is going on right now, in the moment, and at what direction we are heading, then our evolutionary growth takes form. The gap closes, bonding conscious with the subconscious to become one powerful mind.

Gazing upon and being aware of all that is going on around me and in me is calmness. There is neither debris nor baggage, for I am in the flow with life.

Liberation of the Soul

A Return to Divine Light

That which is eternal was lowered down in density to where it lost its eternal grandeur and entered a state of bondage. The deliverance of the human from his self-created bondage, the glory of that which is beyond all grasp of thought, the happiness that is the very foundation of our existence, is nearer to us than anything of a physical nature. It is not a heaven to be experienced after death; rather it is the eternal heaven that is ever present here and now, and always.

—Charlie Lutes

Freedom from Mental Limitations

Liberation we require and liberation we shall achieve, for this is our destiny. We must become solemn about getting out of the denseness and rigidity of mind, for all our self-imposed limitations, our mind-made useless trappings, and our bondage exist solely in mind. We must gain complete access and take residency as much as possible in the void—that space of no thought, of pure consciousness, sacredness, emptiness and light, peace, and immense power.

You may think that to move through your day with no thought is aimless and may cause you to lose your mind, but the opposite is true. In the space of no thought resides the power of the infinite. Know that when your mind is holding a thought, you are in a constant state of chaos. The untruths and judgments cause stress, powerlessness, uncertainty, and strife, all of which are negative and weigh heavily on your being. In contrast, residing in the space of "no thought" gives you an undeniable power, for this is where infinity lives. In this space reside peace, freedom, bliss, and infinite love. In this space of no thought flourishes patience, understanding, creativity, wisdom, and the presence of the self. In this space of no thought are stillness and silence, which bring you into harmony with all that there is.

The self you believe you are and the self that others think you are is not the true self. That is the shallow self you created with mind and called it your personality, which is no more than your idiosyncratic behaviors, wants, preferences, and habits. The true self lies within the space of emptiness, the space of no thought. There you will feel and realize who you truly are. In that space is soul, an infinite being of light. It is here that you will feel and sense the higher realms from whence you came. Here in is found the temple of knowledge, wisdom, and power. It is here that you become one with the universe, for here there is no door, just openness and access to guidance, higher thoughts and understandings, insights, and intuitions. The orchestration of your life will take form from the inside out. It is here that your higher awareness will be formed, which will keep you out of the wallow of erratic mind.

In this space, neither fear nor strife nor doubt can exist, for mind has no control here. In this space, mind becomes accustomed to a divine sense, a presence that allows access to infinite everything, including knowledge, power, love, and peace. You fall into harmony with everything, everyone, and all that there is, including the rhythm of divine light. In this space, you are a different being, for you are at peace with yourself and the world. You can no longer be labeled with personality attributes, for you are "no thing" and "every thing" all at once. You now move through life guided not my mind, but from the realm of possibilities. You have no doubts or fears or presuppositions, for there is no longer any fragility to who you are. You have become definite and purposeful about all your actions and deeds, and your voice and your words resonate your truth forthwith.

Ridding the Ego

Some say that to gain liberation, one must rid oneself of the ego. How does one do this, since ego is mind and mind is here, there, and everywhere? We live in the sea of consciousness and of mind, and mind is necessary for our life, living, and our understanding. Mind, including the ego, is the harbor for our mental and emotional floor plan. We use it for self-identity and our system of belief. It holds our memories and their attached emotions. We use the mind to think, process, create, and imagine. We use mind to interact with others, for it carries the register of who we think we are, such that our identity and our personalities shine through as unique. The ego is the structured part of our personality that includes our intellect, our cognitive functions, our defense functions, and our perceptions about ourselves, others, and the world. The ego helps us organize our thoughts to make sense of them and how they relate to our environment. It represents our reasoning capabilities and our primal drive.

The problem with ego is represented when the ego takes control over our awareness or due to our lack of awareness. In this way, mind (ego) is running our life and we (the awareness) are allowing it, for we are unaware and out of sync with our self. This is living from mind. This is the problem, because when ego is in control, we are unaware that it has taken control and unaware of its veracity. Chaos becomes prevalent, as we are being controlled by a part of us that is self-absorbed and fueled by its own personal (egoist) satisfactions. This process goes against the grain of the salvation we came here to seek.

Rid the ego? You cannot cut it out and discard it, but letting go of its protectiveness, its irrational complexes, and its attitudes may be a better choice. With this faint logic, you will recognize when the ego comes up. You can watch it without giving in to it—without giving any power to it, or indulging in it, or fixating on it. Remember the ego is limited and clearly does not understand the depth of our divinity. Ego does not comprehend that we, the awareness, are divine beings with vast reaches and complexities. Simply watch the ego's responses to situations and then let them go. This is taking your power back. This is giving you the ability to make clear, conscious choices. This is creating a gap for the observer to witness. And the ability to do this easily begins with our awareness. This is the absolute practice in which we must indulge, for letting go of limiting ego thoughts will surely release us in the direction of freedom—free from the rigidity of simple mind and free to experience our true self, our power, and our divinity.

Allow me to be very clear. Our journey in human form here on earth is a journey of spiritual awakening, a journey to self-realization. The largest barrier to self-realization is the ego. The very nature of the ego is separation: you and I are different and we are not the same. It is a daunting concept for the simple mind to bear that we all could be a single unit, functioning as the many, and as long as we are living in simple mind, we will be bound to the proclivities and restrictiveness of human consciousness, which itself is illusionary darkness that hides what is real. There exists an everlasting divide between our mental frame of mind and our true self. There is no truth, freedom, or salvation in simple mind. Our mental attachment to human form binds us forever to the reckoning of karma, locking us into a state of no growth, no freedom, and no salvation. This is bondage where freedom, truth, boundlessness, and divinity are absent. We are misguided to a false sense of self, to the notion that we are born and then we die and that's the end of it, or that we are separate from life. Our only proclivity in this frame of mind is to look outside our self and judge. Where is our deliverance?

Pursuing a material ambition in this life is another way of binding oneself to ego, since material ambitions are typically ego driven. Ego-driven ambitions can never lead to true happiness, for ego knows neither true happiness nor integrity. True happiness cannot be attained through external factors. External ambitions will always wither away, dry up, and disappear. External wants and needs are external to your very being and therefore are impermanent. The fruit of who we are is seeded in the soul. A world exists inside us with the potential to reach infinity. You have a wanting desire to live your divine purpose—that which you came here to deliver. Those deep desires that burn inside you are the very desires of the soul. Those with even a minute awareness will feel the angst of knowing there is something inside them that wants to come to the surface to be expressed into the world—something they feel a strong compulsion to do. Through the will to not do, they have kept that light hidden inside them. As long as we are here on earth, the prodding will continue, for it must. The law of karma is an exacting law, for the scale must be balanced. Expressing your desires into this world is balancing the karmic scale, thus paving the path to redemption of the soul, which invariably moves you toward freedom.

Step away from frail egoic ambitions, for they cannot heal the soul nor lead you toward freedom. By their very nature, they are lacking in permanency, healing power, truth, and divine accord. They are fruitless and will continue to cause you stress and strife in mind and body. They absolutely will not assist in emancipating the soul, nor will the results of shallow desires be fruitful to humanity as a whole. Anything that is not pure of heart and true will keep you bound in the illusion of human frailty.

Within each of us, just beneath the surface and deep within our conscious awareness, there exists a nudge, a desire to know who we truly are and return to the light that is our divine spark. Every man and woman on this planet feels this pull at some point in his or her life, for the light is within everyone, and though you may not be fully aware of it, it burns brightly and will never dim. It awaits your awakening in this lifetime or in other lifetimes to come.

A Shift in Mind

Our journey on earth seems to be moving from being lost to being found; from living in ego mind to recognizing and flowing with consciousness; from thinking we are mere humans to knowing we come from divine light; from being unconscious to gaining wisdom; and from the entrapment of our personalities to seeding into our true divine essence. This is the way to truth, to self-realization, and to returning to the self. However this requires commitment and determination. It requires mental effort and most seem unwilling to foster the effort required. Instead they recline into laziness, which keeps them in simple mind, where they continue to point the finger in judgment of others, of things and situations, without looking keenly within themself. Since the simple mind has no investment in ultimate truth, its judgments come from a standpoint of utter ignorance. One cannot gain wisdom through the practice of falseness and lack of knowledge. The inner work in search of self-awareness must be done or else we continue to wander this earth through countless lifetimes in lack.

In moments when the mind is quiet, some will feel a desire bubble up inside them that cannot be ignored, a sense that there is much more to life than what they have known. This creates a yearning for discovery. This is the psychological junction at which most people discover spirituality. When they confront the depth of these feelings with an inclination to explore, the journey toward the self invariably begins. If they persist, through meditation and stilling the mind, they discover the void—a stillness that is beyond the depth of their imagination and silence so precious they can feel its charged vibrations inside every atom and molecule of their body. In this space, the feeling of love is pervasive and swells inside them, light-years beyond any love they have felt before. In this space, they are cushioned in pure, absolute peace so natural they can almost touch it. In this space, their natural essence of bliss consciousness and harmony emerge and is felt at the deepest level of their being. For the first time in their human life, they realize with absolute certainty that there is significantly more to who they are then previously believed.

This is only their first "feel" of moving their attention toward the light of the self. For abiding in this space will quickly become addictive, since for the first time they realize that there is far more depth to who they are than one could have ever conceived. The realization sinks in that they are not reading a book on how meditation feels. Instead, they are experiencing the void, which is their natural core, and their understanding quickens that they are limitless beings beyond earth and beyond the stars. From this point, there exists an unshakeable movement toward the light. There is no going back. This is not an organized religion where others can lie to them. This is entering the zone of spirit, soul, Atman, and Brahman, and now they know for absolute certainty that they are far more than their human bodies.

As they persist, the simple mind begins to give way to the higher mind, to soul. Stillness prevails, for the glorious journey inward has begun. They quickly discover that a still mind is a treasure point from which all glorious things move. They discover that their innate feeling of calmness, love, harmony, peace, and bliss are being expressed through them even when they are not in meditation—their very being is shifting into the spectrum of higher vibrations. They realize that from stillness arises deeper awareness, spontaneous knowing (wisdom), insights, sharper intuition, and for some, conversations with God. They feel the velvet of the higher mind, the mind of the soul, and the journey to their inner world becomes fortified by the desire to expand their awareness toward the light and to never stop. For the first time, the sight of the soul is in the forefront. As their awareness deepens, their inner journey flourishes in search of absolute truth, understanding, further knowledge, and deeper wisdom. They are assimilating themselves toward the light. All apprehension falls away as the simple mind gives way to the higher mind, and their level of insight and awareness deepens. Their inborn nature to judge, to be hateful and harmful, and to condemn falls away, for now their only requirement is absolute truth. As they move up the consciousness ladder, there is an awareness of "being one with source" that resembles their true nature. They develop an intuitive grasp of truth. They no longer hone the feelings to change others, for they understand that this journey is a journey to the self, for all of humankind. The more they know themselves, the more they understand others.

The ego is diminishing, and now one can concentrate the mind on what things are important and allow the things that are not significant to fall away. Through this natural progression, our lives begin to shift in a new direction. Things become effortless, joyous, peaceful, and harmonious, which is their natural core for moving through life. They have relinquished bad habits and are doing the inner work to clear the baggage of fears, sorrows, and angers that hide in the subconscious mind. This clearing systematically opens the gate to the soul. Ego has not been rid of or killed. It has been put in its rightful place. It is no longer needed, for the higher mind, the soul, is in the forefront and all previous mental, emotional, and psychological loads have been lifted. They have transcended materialism and all earthly illusions; their attention is toward source, and they are moving deeper into divine light. If they remain resolute on their inner journey, they will come to know that they can accomplish anything they believe, for their self-imposed limits have fallen away and they have become ardently aware of their inner power.

This is the power of higher mind.

This is the power of higher vibration.

This is the power we came here to wield.

The Soul

What is soul? Soul is the essence of spirit that is of God. Soul is a divine spark of light from the creator. The soul is the "I" that inhabits the body and animates life into the body. Without the soul, the human body would be an empty shell void of life or intelligence. With the soul, the body becomes alive and springs forth movement, sight, hearing, and the ability to speak. It is the soul that expresses intelligence, reason, and emotion. The soul exercises the will that fosters desires and achievements. The soul is the "I," the self you refer to when you speak of your desires or your identity.

Soul is the engine of your life that delivers the purpose and the significance of our being here on earth. It knows the why of your existence on earth, and it is the substance that moves you in the direction for attainment of its intentions on earth. Most people do not realize that the very thing that drives them, the things they are exceedingly passionate about, the things they love, and the things they have a natural talent for are, in fact, the desires and abilities of the soul. And when you exercise these passions and loves, you are paving the path that is the legacy of your journey. This is the agenda of the soul. Whenever you become lost in an activity that engages you so deeply that time seem to stand still, you are standing in divine light. You are exercising the passion and purpose of the soul.

The soul has been said to have two distinct drives here on earth. The first is for survival, the inborn animal instinct for self-preservation. Once safety becomes apparent, the soul's aim becomes self-improvement: learning, growing, and reaching out beyond perceived limits for advancement. The second is a deep altruistic yearning to reconnect with source, to move back into the light of the divine. To the keen observer, the task of accomplishing both drives may seem improbable. One is earthly focused on physical needs and desires, projected through lower mind. The other is recognition of an inborn light, a subtle nudge that is felt from within, bringing with it an intuitive knowing that there is more than this physical earthly plane with its material life, more that encompasses the whole universe, more that is beyond the physical, and more that is beyond the simple mind they have come to know and trust. Most people spend their lives in pursuit of learning, love, marriage, raising children, advancing their careers, cultivating friendships, engaging in social activities, and trying profusely to fit in. All of these have them grounded in the physicality of life. This becomes their primary focus and all else is pushed to the back. However, it is inevitable, even if it takes numerous lifetimes, that a time will come when that altruistic nudge from within will become so strong that it can no longer be ignored. With this nudge will come the recognition that earthly aspirations and pursuits do not fill the void and the sense of going inside to confront that spark becomes too intense to ignore. For those who do not succumb to laziness relative to the inward looking, the journey toward the light, toward their spiritual legacy, begins.

Why does soul, divine sparks of light, take the journey through denseness and physicality of planet earth? God is the creator of the one life encompassing everything that moves, breathes, flies, and grows. God experiences life through man. Man was therefore created to express the fullness and abundance of God in the world. And to do this, man transcends to the physical realm, clothed in a human body, and must evolve to his God self here on earth, returning himself to the light. For man, fully evolved, becomes the light of God on earth. The fowl in the air, the fish in the sea, the animals that roam, and all other creatures on earth are constrained to follow the natural laws of nature, which is spirit. However, man carries the seed of God and is the only creature given free will, the freedom to choose and decide to obey or not obey the laws of nature. The reason for this is that man was given God's consciousness and will. Man, therefore, must be allowed absolute freedom for the flavor of his own choices and expressions to fully convey God's own freedom.

The nature of man on earth is survival, growth, and to return to source, but the human soul has the substance that divinity is made of. It carries the spark of the creator and therefore plays in the quantum field of pure potential, of limitless possibilities. Let's look at this differently. The "enlightened" soul of man is God on earth. This means that the capabilities of the human soul far surpass its nature for mere survival and expansion. The soul is transformative and can create wonders for humankind. It is the soul's endeavor to create Unity consciousness and Cosmic consciousness on earth. It is the soul's drive to posture love, creativity, beauty, ingenuity, and service, all of which are forms of expressions that connect us to the essential forces of the universe. It is the soul in man that chose not to simply react to his environment but to change it, for his choices and actions are of true consequence to humanity and to life itself. Remember the likes of Buddha, Martin Luther King Jr., Mahatma Gandhi, and Nelson Mandela. They did not simply react to the life they were experiencing. They changed the world.

Incarnations

The soul carries the seed of greatness to be expressed on earth. Every man and woman, therefore, has a divine purpose, a blueprint, for exhibiting his or her birthright by exercising the gifts, the power, and the brilliance that they came to express. The potential of the soul is the potential of the creator.

Behold the soul (spirit), which emerged from the supernal spiritual realm and descended into the coarseness and denseness of earth's lower vibration. Here it clothed itself with the human body (matter), challenged by earthly conflicting needs and desires within, in this arena of hidden truth and perpetual challenges.

It is here that the soul can fully express its divine power, for it has within its grasp the guide to navigate the challenges of physical life on earth.

Yield, therefore, to your soul, for it carries the compass to actualize your earthly destiny.

The soul was never born and it will never die, for it is eternal. It enters the human body when the sperm and the ovum unite and leaves when the human body dies. The soul returns to earth through countless lifetimes, cloaked in varying garments of race, culture, gender, and circumstance, to establish and impart its brand of perfection into the world, to repay karmic debt, and to encourage a return to its spiritual heritage.

On each return to earth, the memories of past lifetimes are erased from the mind of the soul. The soul returns in each incarnation, fashioned with new challenges necessary to suit the passage on which the soul must embark. These passages will always include an assortment of life lessons to be learned through an onslaught of life experiences encroached upon the soul. All are designed to shift the soul into realizing the purpose of its journey and to remember its true self.

The soul cannot know of the purposefulness of these lessons and experiences until it, through its own design, moves toward conscious awareness. Since the soul is unaware of this, it is not aware of its own identity. It believes earth to be its true home and that it is a mere human. The wondering soul, therefore, becomes attached to the physicality of earth. Without the armor of knowledge and memory, it is pulled into the denseness of lower mind. Soul then becomes identified with the five senses, with the intellect and with the body into which it is presently housed. Its divine spark has been forgotten but not lost. Its natural essence of love and harmony and of bliss consciousness remains hidden from it. It feels an innate desire to be happy, and in its newfound ignorance, it seeks happiness through material gain, with its center etched inside the ego mind. So it reaches for more material stuff, finding temporary salvation in money, houses, cars, clothes, or whatever the flavorings of its life stories resemble. It is unaware that it is living from pure ego. It has entrenched itself deeply into human consciousness.

At some point, man is faced with the realization that all of his material gains are temporary and cannot fulfill his innate desire for completeness. Man takes note of that inner light that has been beckoning his return—the light from within him will not go dim. On further investigation, with purposeful intention, he discovers that he must use his will to become familiar with his true self and further evolve the self into the light of divinity. He learns that through stillness and meditation, he can slip into the void and feel his divine essence. He learns that he can free himself from his earthly bondage by becoming the observer of his own self. He realizes that to master materiality, he must transcend it, for by returning to the light, the purpose and desires of the soul become irrevocably possible. He learns that to find his own purpose on earth, he must disassociate from the ego and adapt the higher mind, which is his own self. With this wanting, he notices that many things are shifting inside him as his understanding of the self deepens. He notices less anger and negativity in his stride, less judgment, a sharper desire for wisdom, a yearning to exercise kindness and generosity toward others, and a strong pull to merge back into divine light. There he finds the mechanics to exercise his birthright, which he realizes has always been about love—the love of self and the love of all souls.

Karma

Let's deal with karma here and now, for karma, in itself, is a law that is absolute. There is no getting around it.

Karma is the law of moral and immoral causation or volition. Any kind of intentional action, whether by thought, word, or deed, is regarded as karma. In essence, that which you do returns to you. Although different religious philosophies define karma in different ways, karma implies the eternal struggle between good and evil. Since karma is cosmic in nature, it keeps track of the sum of a person's actions in this life, in past lives, and in lifetimes to come. There is no escaping karma.

We return here in human form lifetime after lifetime with particular experiences and lessons to be learned. These experiences and lessons exist in our energy field and are based on our unpaid karmic debt from previous lifetimes, as well as from the present lifetime. When we face these experiences, which are our greatest challenges in life, and when we interpret them correctly and take the right action, we advance in spiritual awareness, which absolves the karmic debt. In so doing, we unblock an aspect of ourselves of which we were unaware, a part of us that has kept us bound to the past or to ignorance, thus blocking our natural progression to the next level of our evolution. With right action, a door opens, moving us closer to our legacy.

On the other hand, if we do not correctly interpret the experiences and continue to take wrong action, the karmic debts remain in our energy field and additional circumstances come up again and again, giving us the opportunity to take the right action for karmic retribution. In this way, all of our so-called bad experiences or problems are for our own evolution, to propel us forward to our spiritual awakening. When so-called negative experiences show up in your life, look deeply into what the experience is showing you about yourself, your intentions, your habits, or your unconscious follies. Examine the feelings being imparted to you and ask, "What aspects of myself am I being nudged to alter or abandon?"

Some years ago, while being relaxed in stillness, I received a gentle flash of the orchestration of the progression of life on earth. It enlightened my awareness to realize that no matter how "matter of fact" things may seem as our life unfolds, there are no accidents. The movement of our experiences and our growth through life is deliberate and absolute. This flash strengthened my awareness that we are not in control. But fret not, for you are in the hands of absolute perfection and your awareness is all that is required.

During this flash, several episodes or events of my life, that had already occurred, were revealed to me in introspection. These episodes are what we typically refer to as problems. The magic of this revelation was this: the orchestration and flow of all the events of my life were in absolute support of each other, and together in their perfect sequencing, they prepared the route through which I was being led, relative to my unfolding. The realization was that I needed all these episodes to be propelled forward in the life I am meant to live. Therefore, all of the episodes had to come into fruition to move me forward in their perfect sequencing and within their perfect timing. In looking back on these events, I saw absolutely no relation from one to the next. They were all as foreign to each other as a bee to a chimpanzee. But the universe is deliberate and perfect in its orchestration.

The flash revealed that the unfolding of our so-called problems are due to the situations we have unconsciously created through our lack of awareness and knowledge. These experiences happen in our lives to require us to change something about our present habits, such as our lack of knowledge, our irrational thoughts and beliefs, our mental posturing, or our limiting and critical personality traits. They are being delivered to us to identify required shifts in those particular moments in time for our continuous forward and productive movements. When we take the time to look properly at the underlying causes of our situations, we will realize the criteria (habits, thoughts, beliefs, and the like) that we need to alter to create a new mind and to move us away from our current inner state that is stale and must be let go. When we comply, we are creating an internal shift toward a higher mind. The results are newer, more fruitful ways of looking at ourselves, heightened awareness, and recognition that the universe is working on our behalf, as a mother does for her child. Denote nothing, therefore, as a problem. Become the seer of the events of your grooming. Go deep inside and look feverishly for your blockage or the aspects of you that should be released. Allow the mind, through self-awareness, to reveal truth to you, and accept all that is revealed to you with love. Become grateful to your internal guidance system.

Karma itself binds us to this earth plane. For as long as we remain unconscious, we will remain in its grip. Our salvation is spiritual awakening. Keep moving toward the light of the soul, with enlightenment as the final episode to our salvation. Liberation is freedom from mental limitations, from preconceived notions, and from our dislikes and judgments. Liberation is a waking up to the knowing of who we truly are, to our real and true existence. When the veil of ignorance and misunderstanding is lifted through enlightenment, then the true self stands before you. It is you. From here onward, you live from the cosmic energy of the universe, in a cosmic state of mind, which transcends body, mind, senses, and consciousness. You are now free from all limitations and free to live through the signature of the soul. There is no longer any sense of pain or suffering, for your true nature has arrived—that of love. You are the divine mind. You understand your own true self and the world as it is, while remaining detached from the world. There is no further scarring to your evolved mind. It is done. Blissful experiences become commonplace and you become fervently aware that love is the light.

Into the Light

If you have been ardent with your spiritual progress as outlined in this book, you have been readying the soul to return to its divine state. You may very well feel off balance, lost, confused, and unsure of who you are at times, unsure of what direction to move. This can cause you to feel very lonely, but this is good. This is the death of the ego. This is the letting go of all the unconscious paradigms (vain mind stuff) you have held on to for all these years, which were ego-driven creations and therefore of little value to the person you were and of absolutely no value to your spiritual awakening.

By now, you may have emptied out a portion of your subconscious wounds and noticed that some of your fruitless habits and behaviors have simply vanished. Now here you stand, no longer feeling like the self you knew up to this point. It's important to understand though that this is spiritual progress. You have let go of your so-called personality traits and of your loose habits and beliefs that were binding you to earth's illusions, restricting you from any progress toward your true self. You may have recognized the illusions in materiality of this world, recognizing that they were not your salvation, and have let them go. You may have let go of some of your subconscious wounds. Feeling loss is a sign that you have transcended your previous level of consciousness and have moved into higher consciousness. You are letting go of the baggage and illusions of the past and you are moving boldly into divine light. You are entering a newer, fresher, more intelligent state of being, one without the rigidity of personality attributes and earthly beliefs and binds. You have gained some awareness of the self and you are open to the relevance of being awake and aware. You are entering the natural rhythm of life.

Realize also that these episodes of feeling lost will come about several times during your spiritual progress, and as they occur, do the inner work of releasing more of the stored darkness: unprocessed emotions, old traumas, karma, existing distorted beliefs, and childhood wounds that are still resident in your energy field. Feeling lost then becomes the grounds for persevering with the inner work to release anger, sadness, and other subconscious wounds. You are lightening your load. You are readying yourself to enter the light.

It is you, the human awareness, that must prepare yourself to step into divine light. You must open the gate for transitioning from duality (body and mind) to "triality"—the merging of body, mind, and soul into one solitary being. For the first time in your earthly life, all three parts of your self will be working together in unison, in seamless harmony at the same level of vibration, at the same time. All conflicts within you will loosen, because you have gained a sense of balance with your self and with life. Your human desires that previously bound you to the earthly illusions and bondage are falling away, for now, in this more vital state, you are awake to a new paradigm of leaning into the light of the soul for your true earthly purpose. There are no further illusions, for through wisdom, you easily intuit truth and relevance in others, in things, and in yourself. You feel more alive and more connected than ever before. Now look quietly inward to ascertain your soul's purpose for this lifetime and move toward it with your whole self. Your selfless actions will develop your will to endure and persist, and brilliance and love will become the natural out flowing of everything you do.

Entering a Deeper Mind

Man was made in the likeness of God, yet man suffers. It is through man's indulgence in ego mind, and his thwarted thinking and doing, that suffering is caused. Man does not understand the precious mechanics of the body he wears, nor does he comprehend the beauty, wonder, and reach of the mind to which he was granted access. Life is a sacred gift. Nature understands this gift and indulges. Man, with his free will to be and do anything, has, over the ages, become ignorant of the life to which he has a synchronistic bond. The knowledge of this sacred life is being revived in this generation. A deeper and broader energy frequency is upon the earth, and man no longer has to suffer. Man can now redeem himself, for now is the time to enter a deeper mind that is the mind of the soul.

There are seven levels of consciousness designed for man to evolve spiritually, and until they have all been experienced, man will remain distorted, and drowsy. Thus far, man has found only three levels of consciousness: They are:

1. **waking consciousness**
2. **deep sleep**
3. **dreaming**

These three are known to every human who walks this earth. The remaining four levels, however, are to be developed along the spiritual path toward enlightenment and can be gained through transcendental meditation (TM). They are:

4. **Transcendental consciousness**

The mind and the senses rest in completely silent stillness, yet consciousness is fully awake.

5. **Cosmic consciousness**

Once you can abide in and maintain complete silence while busy doing, thinking, moving, and being occupied, the inner silence of the Atman arises in you and stability takes form. A new state of consciousness is born in you, and you see clearly the illusions and the transient nature of the outer world. Everything you previously considered as "me" is now seen as "not me." This is an awakening.

6. **God consciousness**

Bliss deepens and becomes prevalent. Perceptions fall away as you become one with your higher self. You experience deep peace, where subtler levels of awareness are unbound and blissful, and you see joy in everything. You are in a constant state of delight from all experiences in and around you, and you see beauty and perfection in everything. Your devotion is to whatever cause touches your heart deeply.

7. **Unity consciousness**

You have reached the pinnacle of higher consciousness, where your unfolding becomes limitless. This is the full awakening. Now there is no inner and outer, no real and unreal, no self and non-self, no absolute and relative, no eternal and temporal, for there is now only one. There is only one self. One discovers that Atman, which was once inner, is the all and all. Therefore, Atman is Brahman. There is no other.

Transcending to Deeper Mind

As stated by Maharishi Mahesh, "The mind is deep like a lake. The ripples on the surface represent the innumerable activities of the mind, and the whole depth of the lake is silent." The premise is that the depth of the lake represents the subconscious mind, and the deeper you go the more power is inherent. But man does not make use of the subconscious mind. Instead, he remains in the shallow choppy waters of the simple erratic ego mind. However, if man could go deeper into mind, incorporating the more silent levels of mind, then whatever thoughts man is furnishing in mind become far more substantive. If the conscious mind is not in a state of bliss consciousness, which is its essential nature, it will become easily imprinted by the perceptions or thoughts infringed upon it. That is mind still in bondage. When the mind is being overshadowed by the objects of perception, it further loses bliss consciousness. In this case, the object remains (the perception) and the subject (the mind) becomes distorted and lost. A drowsy mind loses eternal bliss at the cost of useless perceptions in this material world. Concentrating on anything within this material world diminishes the soul.

During transcendental meditation (TM), there is a merging of minds. The lower erratic mind merges with the subconscious, which is the higher, supremely infinite mind of the soul, to become one mind. Herein, the choppy surface activities of the conscious mind deepen and become incorporated inside the fold of the subconscious. The whole mind then becomes one conscious mind with infinite potential. This means all your thoughts (erratic or otherwise) and your perceptions will be seen and examined by a more supreme mind. TM takes the mind to a deep level of stillness, into the birthplace, the foundation of thought. TM takes you beyond the thought and into the source of your being. With daily practice, the bliss will maintain itself and is capable of maintaining itself no matter what is going on in your life. You will begin to notice that the erratic nature of your thinking is falling away. You will notice that when you think, your thoughts go deep within, and the responses that reverberate back to your awareness are no less than brilliant. These thoughts will lead to actions that are also the stuff of brilliance, with far less effort. You are becoming polished from the depth of the infinite to which you have become recognizably connected through TM. Your so-called personality will shift to one of calm stillness. You will fret less and will put more care and love into what you do, no matter how trivial. You are touching the light of the soul.

With more practice, you will shift to higher vibrations and move further into the divine light. Subconscious pressure no longer colours your thinking or your outlook on life, for through the infusion of being, you have released and erased these pressures. This raises your vibration and unfolds a new outlook on life. You have plummeted to the depth of silence and have reached the essence of your self; you have become spiritual. You no longer fuss or worry, for you are fully aware of the immense power that is within you. This is spiritual growth, the liberation of your human consciousness into transcendental consciousness. The spirit is not capable of being overshadowed anymore by the objects of your experience. Take many walks in nature and feel your bliss. Watch for subtle moments that take your breath away, which is the emerging of the soul. Recognize life in everything and everywhere.

Advantages of TM

Dr. John Hagletin, Quantum Physicist and teacher of transcendental meditation (TM), states that TM is much more than a meditation technique. TM takes you to the fourth level of human consciousness—Transcendental Consciousness,—a state of absolute stillness.

Advantages of TM

1. TM takes the outward attention of the senses and moves them powerfully inward to experience and explore deeper levels of mind, quieter levels of the thinking process.
2. At this level, mind is complete silence, which is the most powerful antidote for stress and anxiety.
3. TM has profound practical results for our health, our brain development, and our life. It lowers blood pressure more effectively than most hypertensive drugs and much more effectively than other forms of meditation or relaxation. It can unclog clogged arteries. It normalizes insulin resistance, which reduces diabetes.
4. In a nine-year study funded by the National Institute of Health, people with high blood pressure or elevated risk of heart disease experienced a two-third drop in comparison to controls in the number of heart attacks, strokes, and death. TM was more effective than medicine, diet, exercise, and other versions of meditation.
5. The rejuvenated rest of TM also slows the aging process, which can cause people to look twelve to fifteen years younger than their chronological counterparts.

Clearing the Path

By now, you have come to the realization that the only true path is the path to spiritual awakening, to knowledge of the self, to gaining wisdom, and to resurrecting the divine spark of the soul. Now you must evolve the soul. You have become wholly aware that man lives in two worlds: the physical (material) world and the subtle (spirit) world, and what happens in one affects the other. Now it's time to take recognition of the subtle world by exercising right thoughts and actions in the physical world.

Light constitutes all of life and light enters into and through your body and radiates outward. The colour, quality, and vibrancy of your light are directly related to your thoughts, your intentions, and your health. This is your aura, and it carries a protective vibratory charge. Some can see it and others can feel it. Aura is the energy field that surrounds you and is formed by subtle colour radiance. Your thoughts are the emotional expressions of your desires and the radiance of your aura depicts the strength and good intentions of your thoughts, or it depicts dimness and vacancy, which is evident of unworthy motives hidden inside your thoughts. When your health is good and your thoughts are constructive, your aura gives off a high vibration, creating a protective vibratory sphere around you.

Examine your desires and motives. Are they coming from ego mind or from the soul? Are your desires of significant good to you and others or are they shallow and self-serving? Examine them carefully before the internal mechanics of mind harden your shady thoughts, rendering you powerless to alter them after they have become seeded in mind. This is the root of self-mastery and the heart of accessing thoughts before they become wrong action. Repel wrong thoughts and action, for they will distort and weaken your radiance and you will fall victim to negative external habit and environments and internal negative mind forces. Self-mastery is taking charge, becoming the master of your right thoughts, intentions, and actions. This is the discipline that becomes the fulcrum for developing your inner power.

Transcendental meditation increases your vibration. It takes you to a depth of stillness, silence, and power that is beyond the superficial mind. Once there is no choppy, shallow mind with ego or negativity attached, you are using the forces of the subconscious mind, the spark of divine light, to cultivate your desires, thoughts, and forward movements. The only result that will come from this depth of mind is sophisticated thinking, higher processing, and brilliance. With TM, your desires, thoughts, and underlying motives will be of a high vibration and good. Your desire to continue to improve your spiritual awareness and to merge with the soul will create a luminous radiance around you.

Qualities of the Soul

Actualize your goals, for the heart-print of God is in the doing. The doing increases and polishes your service to humankind and prepares you for a time when you can use your natural abilities to generate an income. But in the here and now, give it away. You may have heard the statement that humans are not perfect. That may be true when we are blind and lost in the paradox of lower mind. But when one stands in the power and affluence of one's natural abilities and is touching the hearts and minds of those bearing witness, one is said to be perfect. Human perfection then is the ability to touch the hearts of others in a fruitful and blessed way by standing in your element, exercising your grace with the gifts you bare. This is optimal service to humanity.

When your actions are serving others, you are balancing the karmic scale. Don't get me wrong: your karmic scale is definitely heavier on the side of sin, which is why we will continue to reincarnate here for countless lifetimes until the karmic scale is balanced. There are those who believe we will never be able to completely balance the scale, because we indulge in sin every day. But doing good begets more good until all your unwholesome trysts have evaporated and your service and your good nature become your fruit—soulfully giving and loving.

You are building your bridge to the soul. Look around. Who else can you help? As long as you have the abilities to help, perfect it. You will find that as you give, your giving becomes easier, until you don't know how not to be of service. Live the doing and love those whose life you are affecting. Become present in the doing and feel the energy of service swelling around you. You are moving gallantly along the continuum of soul. A continuum is a sequence in which adjacent elements are not perceptibly different from each other, although the extremes are quite distinct. Soul qualities begin with feelings of *contentment,* and when contentment intensifies, one feels *happy*. When happiness intensifies, one feels *thrilled* and then *overjoyed,* moving to *ecstatic* and then *blissful*. Each one builds on the one before, moving us along the path to our higher evolution toward the natural essence of soul.

Feeling ecstatic or blissful are qualities that may occur in moments of subtlety. These are moments in which you may feel as if you are having an out-of-body experience, as if you are watching yourself from outside yourself and feel as if you are not in control of your movement or whatever it is you are moving toward or gazing upon. This is so because, as your vibration heightens and you continue to move along the continuum, the soul takes over and begins to move you toward noble actions or services of a gallant nature—and toward bliss consciousness, which is your very essence. This can feel as if you are receiving a guided push, since you may not have made up your mind to follow the nudge, yet here you are moving in its direction. It may also feel as if someone or something was moving your body, speaking through your lips, or looking at something that you had not previously noticed.

These moments will catch you off guard, and the feelings that come from these experiences are pure bliss. One moment in bliss may feel like one hour in earth time, because during the experience, you are lost in time; you have transcended time. When you come out of that sacredness of being, you will know that you have had a glimpse of the depth of soul. Your awareness will deepen as you grasp the efficacies of being present in every moment, knowing the wonders that can come of it. Subtle moments give you a glimpse of your essence, observed through the eyes of the one experiencing soul. These experiences bring something vital to your development. They bring an absolute knowing, not a wondering, nor a believing, nor a hoping, but a substantive absolute knowing. This knowing increases your depth of awareness and brightens and deepens your commitment to your purpose. You are quenched with the wisdom of the magnificence of your true nature; you have a deeper appreciation for who you are, and you become aware that you are making discernable progress along the continuum.

On a very bright and sunny day in the summer of 2010, I came to a heavily trafficked intersection in downtown Toronto. It was noontime, but if you didn't know that, you might have thought it was rush hour. The intersection felt heavy and noisy and bullish, with a dense scent of fumes and chaos. The stoplight changed to green for the pedestrians and I started across, heading southbound. I noticed an older lady, possibly in her eighties, in the intersection heading northbound. I knew from her hunched-over movement and slow pace that she would not make it to the other side before the light changed. I thought that I would take her by the hand and lead her across to ensure her safety. Very quickly, mind revealed its case to my awareness. *If she does not want the help, or if she does not like me, she may scowl, leaving others to think I may be harassing her.* So with that thought, I decided not to approach her.

What happened next became a moment in time. I saw my body moving boldly toward her with a graceful smile on my face. And in a most charming tone, I said, "Hello, I will help you across." She immediately said, "Thank you so much." I reached down and took her right hand and gently placed it on top of my left hand, and then I turned to move in the direction she was crossing, moving at her pace. As I had predicted, the traffic light was changing as we took our last two steps to safety. This gave the motorists traveling in an east-west direction the provision to go through the intersection. But something else happened: No one moved. The entire intersection froze. This intersection is one of the busiest intersections in down town Toronto, frozen in time through the grace of Spirit. The heaviness and noisy bullish sound of the intersection fell into a hush. The fumes vanished. All eyes turned to us: motorists, people on foot, people on bicycles and motorcycles, and vendors. In that moment the entire intersection became transfixed in the phenomenon, as if there was no traffic, no noise, no heat, no hurry, and no time. The entire intersection became pulled into this expression of love. A purity of stillness that I could never have imagined pervaded this place for all in eyeshot to see, feel and experience. Time ceased in order to allow this moment to be realized. The effects of that moment are still resident in me. What may have been one minute of earth time felt like twenty minutes of heaven's radiance, with the grace of goodness raining down on all who had been ushered into that moment and captivated by its spell, for no one moved. All eyes were fixed in a gaze, frozen in time, enthralled by this divine experience. It was as if their bodies had to become still so this moment of divine grace could be impressed upon their hearts and minds. We had all become one, arrested in a single breath of time and space. Everyone just watched, all embossed in the unfolding of divine grace. I raised her right hand to my lips and gently kissed it. She said, "Thank you so much," her voice polished with grace. She reached her arms up around my neck, hugged me, and kissed my cheek. We had all just experienced an infinite moment in time.

This example is what is meant by the soul taking over. My lower mind made its case and I quickly complied. But soul took the reign and expressed its essence for all to experience. In that moment in time, I felt love for self, love for my lovely crossing partner, love for everyone invited to share in the experience, and love for the stillness and blessedness of that moment. We are all drenched in love when we are in the experiences of subtlety. This is the degree of love that lives in us, just waiting to be expressed into the world.

Love is not about the giving of big and flashy things or large sums of money. Giving love is good, and it is simple. Feel love in the moment and express what you feel. Smile at someone just because. Call someone just to say, "I am thinking of you." Help those who need the help that you can provide. Send loving energies to those who are not well. Use your gifts and abilities to enhance the lives or the experiences of others. Love is the pleasant thought you hold about someone. Love is the gentle nod you impart to someone as you pass him or her on the street, just to say, "I see you." Love is looking directly into someone's eyes as you chat, for in the iris is where the soul can be seen and felt.

As you grow in your grace, the vibrant iridescent lights that radiate from the subtle bodies, your aura, will hold and express the degree of love you encompass from within. The more radiant the light, the more impact you will have on others, uplifting them and even healing those in your depth of field. You are becoming a light in the world. You will attract others with similar light. Your inborn power will burgeon outward as your goodness populates in the here and now. This is spiritual progress, and it is all about love.

Outside Time and Space

After the breakup with my fiancée in 2004, I decided to take a break from relationships. I had never really had much space between relationships, so this time, I willed myself to take a substantial break. Approximately two years later, around January 2006, a readiness resonated up through me and into my awareness. The feeling from within was that I was ready again for a committed relationship, even though I was still having some issues with my memory and concentration and parts of my "executive functioning" were not totally aligned; nonetheless, I decided to look for love. For the first time in my life, I got on a dating site. What happened next shocked me at first, but I quickly fell into the rhythm of the unfolding, becoming the watcher of divine happenings. This will give you a glimpse into the gleam of possibilities when we become aligned with consciousness.

I developed the verbiage for my online profile, using simple words and being very direct. I advised that I was on the spiritual path and was looking for someone who was also on that same walk. Within a few days, I had received interest from several women. As I looked through these profiles, something became apparent. I had been contacted by several women who were on the spiritual walk, but whom also seemed quite demanding from the get-go. I will quote a few.

- "Please take a look at my profile and call me immediately."
- "Here is my number. Call me ASAP."
- "I think we know each other. Call me."

In all cases, they provided their phone numbers, which was unusual. Most people communicate first through the dating site's network to ensure trust and the probability of a potential match, before they commit to passing along their e-mail and their phone number. But these women preferred to skip the usual introductory stages, jumping directly to immediate phone contact. I remember looking at the profile of Mila. There were not many words in her profile and five pictures, but after looking at the first photo, I felt nothing and exited her profile. The next day, I received another message from Mila. She stated, "Please take a look at my profile." So again I looked, but this time I looked at the second photo. Still, I felt nothing, so again, I exited her profile. On the third day, there was yet another message from her, asking to please look at her whole profile—almost as if she knew I did not look at all her pictures. So this time, I did. I looked at picture number three—still no feeling. Then number four—still nothing. And now I arrived at the last picture. This picture was a close-up, and for the first time, I saw her eyes, and I was held in a state of shock. I was looking deep into something that was very familiar. I could not look away.

Something drew me into her, as if I was hypnotized. I felt many things, some quite confusing. There was a deep sense of familiarity, a knowing. There was something hypnotic, a pull that came from deep within me. I reached for the phone immediately and called the number, and she answered. She began to speak, and something unusual was happening inside me. So I interrupted. "Who are you? I don't know you, but I know that I do know you. What is this? What is going on?" I was puzzled yet very intrigued, for in her voice was a signature, a resonance that I completely recognized. I knew it well and was positive of this knowing. Yet I was also aware that I had never heard that voice in this lifetime.

She laughed when I asked who she was and, she stated immediately that we should meet. Mila was well on the spiritual path and very dedicated to it. We spared no time and met at a café.

When I first saw her, mind popped up to let me know that "I" was not attracted to her, but mind was quickly overshadowed and put to rest because I was drawn into her. I could not take my eyes off her, as if wanting to look straight through her. We were intertwined in a knot that needed to be unraveled for the sake of not going crazy. Through the eyes of soul, she was radiant and picturesque and I wanted her. So I kept asking, "What is this?"

Her awareness seemed sharper than mine, for she advised that it is possible that we have been together as a couple in other lifetimes. Up to that moment, I was unaware that souls, having romantic fellowships in past incarnations, could recognize each other through the eyes, but the awareness in me was awake, alert, and ready to explore. Later, we asked a psychic friend to advise us and were told immediately that we were married in a previous lifetime. Apparently, I was a Chinese inventor and she was my Japanese wife and we were deeply in love. What was interesting about this was that in this lifetime, I have always felt something quite captivating about the Japanese female. In my frame of reference, there is an allure, an angelic sweetness about them. There are no accidents.

Mila in this lifetime is Italian. We spent time together talking, being, and trying to pull apart history through incarnations and into the present time. The air around us was cluttered with intense feelings beyond anything I thought was possible. When looking into each other's eyes, we felt the power of love, big gaping love, percolating inside us, moving like wine through a straw, slowly and hypnotic, trancelike. I asked the divine in me if through this meeting, and our past experience of love, are we to be together in the here and now. The response was this: because we have been lovers before, it does not mean that we should be lovers in this lifetime. What I was not aware of was that this was only the beginning of what was in store for me, relative to experiences beyond the limits of the imagined.

The second person I met was a professional jazz singer who had traveled Canada, the USA, Europe, and the West Indies. When we met in person, the same feelings of intensity, of deep allure, were in the air. But there was no further shock because I adapt quickly. I realized that the love was already there, for when souls fall in love, it is not for a moment or for a time. It transcends time and space. So the intensity of what we were feeling was alive and very real. But allow me to skip to the third lady, for based on probabilities, this one was supposedly impossible, except for the fact that it happened.

I called the third lady, knowing that this experience would be different from the others. Thus far, each experience had brought something profound. Through these meetings and prior experiences, I could sense that I was being familiarized with the extent of possibilities and probabilities, and that each would bring something I could not have experienced before in this life. I had already been shocked and adapted quickly.

Our first long-distance chat lasted for four hours. The moment we heard each other's voice on the hello, we began to laugh. Not a blaring laugh but a laugh with a resonance that says, "I know you from the depth of my being" so words are not necessary.

The systematic laughter went on and on for a while, and within each stanza of laughter, we understood each other's feelings and mind-set and excitement perfectly. When we began to speak, it was obvious that through this extraordinary recognition of each other, through voice reverberation and a deep sense of unity, we had a definite and very deep connection. Why do I say this? Because from the very first words spoken, we were finishing each other's sentences. How was this even possible? For example, at one point, a thought popped into my mind. I said, "I just had a thought."

She said, "Yes, you want to go on a hot-air balloon ride."

"And how the heck do you know that?" I asked.

But it didn't matter, for that went on and on and on, until we accepted the fact that we were meticulously connected as one. We told our entire life stories to each other, and everything paralleled throughout: how we see ourselves in this world, how we have the same gifts and abilities to impart to humanity, how we discipline our kids with the exact same mind-set, and how we have schoolings in multiple disciplines. All of this we have used or are still using to foster different careers and our own businesses. This includes how we are viewed by others in the exact same way.

On the third day of conversing, we both started sniffling at the exact same time. She stated that she must have caught something from one of her children who was in junior school. Nonetheless, we both developed a "cold" in the same instance in time, and exactly three days later, while talking on the phone, the cold disappeared from both of us at the same moment in time. There were other exacting and intense things that happened to both of us in parallel, but I dare not put them in this book. Although we both realized that we were bound together, we did not understand why or how, but we accepted that somehow, in some way, we were the same infinite being: one male and the other female but exact duplicates. We were one.

I spoke to others and did some research of my own and the compilation of findings suggest there is a theory that souls come in twins or in halves—two halves make the whole. The notion is that one half typically comes to the third-dimensional earth and the other half would venture to a dimension other than earth—never the two halves are in the same dimension at the same time. They rejoin when they return home. But the research indicated that due to the resident problems placating planet earth, such as excessive environmental issues, global financial crisis, poverty, global warming, racism, and war, both halves of twin souls come to this third-dimensional world. Their combined powers carry more weight to deter some of the rubbish being postulated by man.

It was an amazing experience to meet my other half in the here and now. Through our long and deep conversations, and through learning our exactness, it became very clear that we were two parts of the same Self. It was also clear we wasted no time in honing the gifts with which we came. We did not spend time holding on to one career or becoming mediocre. We had been using all the abilities we came here to seed. We used them to excel at our vocations and businesses, to assist others to a brighter life and learning, to reveal to others what is possible, and simply to help whenever and wherever we could. We are ferocious in our plight to keep moving, growing, and shining the light. I have met my twin soul, which delivers more truth and deeper awareness than I could've imagined, and I feel blessed.

This was so highly improbable that it was almost impossible, but look again. These experiences are telling us that nothing is impossible when you walk in the light and with the light that is your true self. Getting to know yourself is the only true beginning of your earthly abode. Stepping into the light of your true self creates your heaven on earth.

I met Heika shortly after meeting my twin soul and I felt as if all the previous experiences had guided me to the recognition that possibilities are endless and that there is no limit to love.

I tried speed dating for the first time: ten men, ten women, and ten minutes with each person. When I sat in front of Heika, time slowed, for we fell into a hush, a quiet lull, as if we were looking inside each other rather than looking at each other. We did not speak very many words, for a feeling of infectiousness was abound—a perpetual smile planted graciously on our faces and we were never glancing anywhere else. We were just constantly looking and feeling deeply, the smiles never leaving, the energies between us holding in what felt like a quiet solace. When the ten minutes passed, I knew—I just knew—I wanted to spend the rest of my time on earth with this goddess, so we chose each other. On our first date, we went out to dinner and what became apparent very quickly was the energy vibration between us. The longer we sat, the deeper the energies grew, accompanied by a perpetual smile that never left us for a moment. Time must have stopped, for we did not remember ordering, eating, or seeing anyone else that evening. With fingers touching and later hands clasping, eyes never stopped looking deeply, bodies excited, we became completely lost in time.

There was nothing usual about us together. There were no usual dating protocols being exercised either. We started spending most of our time together from the get-go. We admitted, after a few days, that we were completely in love with each other and had never felt this way before, nor knew such depth of love existed. The vibrations fell in place so fast that it was almost unreal. The energies around us were attracting others as well. One evening while walking on the boardwalk near the lake, we fell into a trance where several minutes became lost. When we returned to consciousness, we had been engaged in a kiss so deep that the memory of it was not yet entrenched in our awareness. But what we noticed were several onlookers, some couples and some older women, standing there looking on, melded in the moment. They were transfixed as if stuck on an illusionary drug, their smiles endorsing as if they had seen something akin to their heavenly dreams. They were feeling the bliss and became irrevocably pulled into the infectiousness of the moment, as if it belonged to them. In essence, they were sharing in the moment, for bliss is infectious and draws others to it. Their eyes told a story. Some, still smiling infectiously, nodded and moved on, while others remained standing, still transfixed in awe. We were told by other strangers that they could feel the fullness of love between us from a distance.

I had been in love before, but this love was more powerful than anything I had felt or knew existed. It was beyond our comprehension, yet it was easy. It required no effort and no attachment to it. It was akin to being taken up and carried by the wind, where no effort on our part was necessary. Everything that came from it was new—never before felt or imagined—but bold and easy like the wind itself.

The love didn't stop there. It had deeper revelations for us. Our intimacy felt as if it too was alive. A touch of her skin would bring forth feelings of sweetness, as if my hands had changed places with my tongue. But this sweetness was sweeter than any sweetness the tongue has ever tasted. It was beyond the sweetness you have known your whole life. And the contagion of her natural scent was felt in and through me like dewdrops through cotton. Everything everywhere felt as if I were inside her entire being, as if melded together where two become one. Drawing her closer, a kiss took us into the supernal realm—sacred, enigmatic, and precocious, bound in an everlasting vacuum of oneness so tight yet supple, soft, and sweet. Her taste and the rapture of her gracious nectar would rush through me like air through a vacuum, the extraordinary sweetness percolating through my veins, skin, heart, bones—everywhere—merging us further into one solitary being, one rhythm, one estate, one bliss.

What I felt, she felt, for we were one. The feelings were more delightful than paradise, throbbing through us as we breathed in the same air. And once all movements ceased, we dared not move, for the flow might begin again on its own terms, as it did in most instances. In this embrace, time did not exist. There was only this moment and the one after, and a sense of no end. We were involved in something that belonged where angels soar, for there was nothing of earth in any of this. On earth, we talk about "cloud 9" as being the epic of sexual ecstasy. Then in just representation, this was in the atrium of "cloud 2009." We were eternal beings in the rapture of everlasting bliss. And when the intimacy subsided, bliss was still afloat for many hours. These words I am using are mere fragments of the words to be used, except such words do not exist in the English language. Each moment felt truly like heaven, for earth has no such thing.

This love and its intimacy were beyond the senses of earth. This belongs in a place far, far away, where heaven lives, thrives, and blossoms. But since we never left this place, then heaven is right here where we are. Heaven is a state of being, a state of allowing, and a state of unblemished oneness. When you have touched heaven, that place of purity and of divine light within you becomes alive. Understand that since love is felt in the heart, the most sacred place on earth is within the hearts of man. Rest there when you can.

The orchestration of life is absolute. There are no errors when two people come together. It may feel to you that you went out and found true love, but know that everything is woven perfectly by spirit, without room for errors or accidents. The gem in relationships is whether we learned from the union or not. Heika and I came together to experience the immensity of love and the container it placed in our hearts for holding the experience beyond linear time. Our consciousness rose above what most take for granted. We were lifted beyond the realm of what we thought was possible and now we understand that life is unpredictable and flavorful, and now we know that anything and everything is possible. While we are in physical form on earth, there exists the duality of life by which we must abide. For example, where one encounters love beyond the imagined, that love also brings with it something of the opposite, that being a problem or an issue to be solved of the same strength and degree that the love bore. There are no mistakes; there are no errors. The paradox is that the universe brings people together to heal each other. This is what souls do for each other. They reveal to each other what lives inside the one observing. If both people are consciously aware, they will recognize what issues live inside them that must be healed now for their own evolution in the form of heightened awareness.

Heika had daddy issues, and I had mommy issues. Interestingly, I was not aware of my having mommy issues at the time, but I was very aware of her having daddy issues. Thus, the nature of both our issues, and our blindness to them created a train wreck waiting to happen. The veracity of the love we shared held us together for well over four years, but since neither of us was being healed, the problems instigated by our childhood traumas remained. If you had asked either of us at the time, how many issues we had in the relationship, we both would have said one. Although I was spiritually aware, Heika was not, and in fact, she did not believe in God. Therefore, any assistance from a spiritual teacher or healer was out of the question for her.

When we finally decided to part, we both professed to each other that the love was still there in its powerful form. A few months later, she advised that she did not know how to get past this love, for it was still there. I, on the other hand, had already accepted that this love was to stay with me. I knew it would remain in my energy field, and I relished the times when through thoughts of her, or remembrances of something we did or felt, the love came rushing back into my awareness. I did not mind, for I intuitively understood that such love would last beyond time and space. Some weeks later, she asked if we could try again to be a couple, and naturally I said yes. We tried, and again it failed. Several weeks later we tried again, and again it failed—same problem, same ignorance of not recognizing how to solve it.

I will share something else with you about our togetherness. In this lifetime, Heika is from Switzerland. Her lovely features were quite striking and somewhat exotic. While in relationships, I sometimes refer to my lover with cute nicknames. So when I wanted her attention, I would say, "Hey, German." And yes, I knew that Switzerland and Germany were two different countries, yet even though she asked me to stop calling her German, those words would roll off my tongue every time. One day I decided to ascertain why the word *German* kept slipping off my tongue. Through meditation, I quickly slipped into the void, and when I was immersed in pure spirit, I did not need to ask the question, for I was taken back in time, through what is referred to as past-life regression. There I was, a general in the German army, in uniform and wielding incredible power. But allow me to get to the point. Heika was my beautiful German wife. We had two beautiful children and we lived a gracious life together until the end of our days. In that lifetime, I also liked the use of nicknames for the ones I loved. And for Heika, my wife, I would say, "Hey, German."

Heika and I had been together before. Calling her "German" was the recognition of a past life and love, a love that was reconnected in this present incarnation, creating a bigger than life energy around us and in us. I have no doubt we will meet again, for this powerful love is the beacon through which we will find each other again in other incarnations. I am sure of it. Now you know that love transcends linear time, and if both parties recognize the love through being consciously aware, the bigger, broader, and deeper the energies will flow. I trust that my awareness will continue to grow in this lifetime and in the ones to come. Namaste.

Experiences such as these are revealing to us that we are touching the soul. When our awareness multiplies, we move to higher states of being. In essence, we slowly become aligned with soul and take on soul qualities. Inside these experiences, the self is standing outside time and space. We have transcended the dimensions of earth, even though our physicality remains here on this plane. These experiences are also revealing to us that it is soul that carries the memories of love through countless lifetimes, for it is soul that recognizes those with whom it has had romantic fellowships or family ties through other lifetimes. Know that most, if not all, people in your lives—family, friends, acquaintances, etc.—are souls with whom you have spent many lifetimes. The saying is that souls travel in clusters. Thus, most of the people who make up your circle of family, friends, or influence are souls with whom you have been traveling through countless lifetimes. And be aware that distance is of no consequence to the soul.

I met Lorraine online on a Neale Donald Walsh seminar. The seminar was eight weeks and had many people from all corners of the world online at the same time—some via phone and others through the Internet. On the second day of the seminar, a woman from Ireland asked a question to the broad audience on techniques for stilling the mind. Five people posted answers on the website and I was one of them. Two days later, she posted directly to my name that she had tried them all and my suggestion worked best for her. I wrote back to say thanks and we both felt a connection through the writing. We exchanged e-mails and began e-mailing each other throughout the seminar and thereafter. It became evident very quickly that there was something peculiar between us. We both felt a connection, an inkling of familiarity with each other. I told her that I felt a strong protectiveness toward her. We both decided to find out what this was, so I asked my psychic friend who is able to read the Akashic records to have a look. I sent her a picture of Lorraine and she immediately got back to me, stating that we were young lovers in one lifetime and I was her father in another lifetime. The protectiveness I was feeling was that of a father for his daughter. We have remained friends since then and still communicate regularly.

Here is a grand manifestation from halfway across the globe. In July 2014, I made a decision to find a romantic partner and this time my intentions were very specific. I wanted to find love with a Japanese woman. As I mentioned before, I have always had a warm spot for Asian women, and most preferably, Japanese. Even that preference tells you something about my incarnations. I may have spent many lifetimes in a Japanese or Asian skin. However, I got onto a website that catered to people looking for cultural exchanges, learning new languages, travel partners, and relationships with others of different cultures. I set up a profile, but I did not pay to join. In essence, I could not really communicate with anyone. I was only able to send and receive smiles.

Three weeks later, I received an e-mail from the gentleman who runs the website. He stated that a Japanese woman had seen my picture and profile and wanted to get in touch. I looked at her pictures and noticed that not only was she quite lovely, but I felt a familiarity. I accepted the invitation and our information were exchanged to each other. We communicated first by e-mail. Her English was possibly 2 percent. She knew only about twenty-five English words, and I knew no Japanese, but through our struggling communication, many things were revealed. The first was she chose to meet me after seeing my profile and picture because, as she put it, "Your eyes, your eyes, I recognize."

Things got more bizarre as we communicated. By the second week of this very uncanny communicating, we were feeling deep love for each other, like a man would love his wife and a woman would love her husband. We were exactly alike, aligned in every way that a man and a woman can be aligned. Even our likes and our desires, and our fetishes of what romance should be, were the exact same. I even noticed that her writing, even in its broken state, had the exact rhythm as does my writing. I advised her that she was also a writer like me. She said, "No, I cannot. I cannot."

During that same week, Aki held a seminar where government officials and those involved in maintaining the Japanese culture, including some from the Japanese public media, were present. Her business and pastime is teaching Japanese young women about the Japanese culture, in hopes of maintaining it. At this event, she was approached by one of the top representatives of a Japanese magazine who asked her to begin writing one-page articles for them on a monthly basis. She later advised me that under no circumstances would she have accepted, because she was not a writer. But based solely on the fact that I had told her she was a writer, she accepted. It was as if we were conjoined through love, through thought, through sameness in desires, and through feelings of the heart, for there was an indelible harmony between us.

Again, I sent one of her pictures to my psychic friend and asked her what she sees of Aki and me. Again, she called back immediately to say that I have spent many, many, many lifetimes with this one. She stated that we have been siblings, we have been best friends, we have been lovers, and in a recent lifetime, possibly the one before this present time, we were married. Is that not bizarre that we met, since we have lived all of this life on opposite sides of the globe? No. There is nothing bizarre about the unfolding of life, for through spirit, our life unfolds. This is the power of accessing the qualities of the soul. Aki flew to Toronto to meet me. It was complete bliss sharing time with my wife from another life.

In this incarnation alone, I have met and become aware of twenty-two souls with whom I have had past lives. And the numbers keep growing. Just last week in one of my spiritual meet-up circles, one of the members and I became aware that we were brother and sister in a past incarnation and husband and wife in another. In the here and now, we are very playful with each other. And the memory came through that we were exactly as playful in our past incarnations. A few weeks later I became aware that two others in the circle had been one, my wife and the other, my sister in the same previous lifetime. My mother in this incarnation has been my mother in a number of incarnations. I have met two of my brothers from past incarnations. All others were my wives/lovers.

So why do most people not realize that their mother has been their mother or their sister in past lifetimes? Or that their best friend has been their husband or wife in previous lifetimes? To look in someone's eyes and see and know that you have connections in previous incarnations comes from a deeper awareness arising from merging with the energies of the soul. The deeper and broader your awareness, the more spacious you become, opening you to many subtle experiences that will hold you in their grasp. For you to fully partake in this, you must evolve the conscious mind. This is the only way to live a fully conscious life.

When the conscious mind is evolved, it comes into alignment with the subconscious knowing, causing you to see more clearly and to make decisions based on that seeing, and to know deeply what is happening inside you and around you. The dust is being removed from your mind's eye, for the subconscious is the driver of our life. It is the subconscious mind (the mind of the soul) that carries the timetable of all our experiences to be had on earth. It is through the subconscious mind that our life unfolds. The conscious mind on its own has no part in this and, therefore, is always running behind, trying to catch up with what is going on in you and around you.

The noise or confusion you feel inside your mind is the conscious mind trying to figure out what just happened, akin to always looking out the rear window in a moving vehicle. You cannot use the conscious mind to find answers. You must allocate answers through the subconscious, through meditation, or through awareness that comes from stilling the mind. All the people in our life are a part of our soul cluster, even the ones in different countries. But you cannot recognize souls from past incarnations through the conscious mind. You must rest in the mind of the soul, the higher mind. This is from where will come your grandest realizations that you are spirit. When the conscious mind becomes evolved, the playing field becomes leveled and now all of mind is working on our behalf. Thus, we will be living through divine leadership, through powerful insights, intuitions, subtle experiences, and wisdom.

There is only one love, and that's all there will ever be. When you love, you either love completely without fragments or your love is not true. If you love with conditions, the love is not true, for true love has no conditions and therefore no boundaries. When your love is void of attachments, boundaries, or obligations, then you can feel the power of true love, which will take you into the sacred realm. When your love for another is through friendship, love channels itself one way through the body. When your love has romantic inclinations, love channels itself a different way through the body, for there is only one love. Love outside of consciousness in not true love, for it is infected with mind, attachments, and other mental requirements and conditions. Raise your level of awareness and prepare to merge with soul, to gain access into the realm of infinity.

Pay particular attention to your inner self. What qualities are brewing inside you or have already matured in you that were previously absent? Have the feelings of *compassion* arisen within, replacing the likes of judgments and contempt? Do you feel your *strength* from deep within and hold no doubts about your forward movements and your capabilities? Do you recognize *truth* when you hear it and are you in acceptance of only truth, both from yourself and from others? Do you have moments of pure *bliss* for no describable reason or from seeing things in their glory for the first time? Do you naturally see *beauty* in others and in things, abstract or not, and do you relish in that beauty? Do you feel *love* radiating outwardly, love for others and for the moment, such as watching a flock of geese in uniform flight? Has your *wisdom* deepened? Do you feel the infinite speaking directly through you? Do you feel wrapped in your natural *power* and know that you are capable of anything?

These are soul qualities that will mature as you move gracefully along the continuum, each one building upon the one before, moving you deeper into the essence of soul. The presence of these qualities is therefore the recognition of your spiritual deepening. Pay attention to all the things that strike your attention in profound ways, or that invoke feelings of love and gratitude. When you can be struck with astonishment or become humbled by the simplicity of things that would typically go unnoticed, you are maturing into the true essence of soul.

Love radiates. Love ushers. Love is the light.

Self-Mastery

Life is a most beautiful gift and we must honor it by how we project ourselves into the world. How you project yourself into the world must come from a strong base, cultivated from the inside, resonating outwardly your true essence of love, peace, and harmony. Self-mastery begins with changing your state of mind. You must conquer the enemy from within—the ego mind. The ego mind has set forth a myriad of limitations, blocking us from seeing the nature of our true self. We must take responsibility to move beyond ego and beyond our self-created limits. For what lies in wait is freedom—freedom from artificial confines and freedom to finally see and know who we truly are, which is Atman, bliss, love, soul—all one and the same. This is the liberation of the soul of man.

- Cultivate an attitude of oneness. Look into the eyes of everyone to whom you speak. See and feel their essence. See God in all.
- Remain in the vibration of peace. It is a sphere of influence that promotes healing and understanding and is the grounds from which springs happiness and oneness.
- It is not a given situation that is bad or good. It is your reaction to it that judges it to be so.
- Go into the darkness to see the light and experience who you are.
- Put yourself in the place of others with empathy. Observe, but do not judge. Be at peace, always. See the good in all situations.
- Life moves. It is the law of change. Move with it. Find your own destiny.
- Do not let down anyone or let your grace fall away. Do not interfere in people's lives or tarnish their personalities.
- See with the third eye, the center point of everything.
- See what you should see and not what you are looking at.
- Develop caliber, quality of character. It makes a difference. Find your soul. Soul is the source of your caliber.
- Do not walk into any situation or action that does not enhance your grace.

- Every relationship is based on one thing: each individual's emotional security.
- Learn to take care of the body. It is the sensory system for the soul.
- Conquer the mind from negativity, from ill thoughts, and from your lower self.
- Don't seek sympathy from others. It means you lack self-respect. It means you are begging.
- Be careful what you say, for once you utter something, the vibrations are out.
- God's promise to each soul is that you will meet your teacher for a moment. In recognition of the teacher, which comes in many forms, you either work it out or you don't. Choose to obey or disobey.

Various sources

Burgeoning

Now you are beginning to see the effects of meditation. It has taken you from erratic and inconvenient behaviors to a calm stillness from within. Your desire to merge with soul is paramount, and you can feel the divine spark rising in you. There are moments in which you feel your own essence of truth, of pure joy, and being firmly present in the now. Any thoughts of causing harm to anyone have been pushed outside you. Even wanting to harm an insect will diminish. In fact, you may recognize that your fears of insects have passed. You look at all living things as treasures on earth. You are recognized for the things that are important to you, that are your purpose, and you move with ease toward them. You have clarity that you are not the body, the mind, the senses, or the ego and begin your detachment from them, relative to your emerging true self. You no longer feel stress or strain about life or anything that happens in your life, for you know the veil of bondage and illusions have been cast away and you see things for what they are. You are becoming more detached from worldly objects and more attached to the delight of your spiritual growth and the magnificence that will come from your awakening.

Many of your previous automatic actions and habits that were based on ego have subsided and are now being replaced with selfless actions, which brings more peace, joy, patience, and gratitude into your self. You feel what is happening inside of you, for you are transforming even without trying; you are entering the light of the soul. You are of a higher mind, of higher thoughts and more fruitful actions. You begin to feel subtle moments that stop you in your tracks, such as the radiance of a sunset or the sculpture embossed within the clouds, fashioned by the hands of God. Even the wind feels different as it caresses your skin. You are able to notice these things because worry, sorrow, and distractions are quietly vanishing. This leaves room for feelings of joy, such as seeing things through the mind of the soul for the first time. You are realizing and learning more about yourself daily, and this deepening feels pure and natural. In retrospect, you see the ego for what it is: the gatekeeper to bondage.

As you continue to meditate and your good actions and thoughts become natural, your evolution increases. Your evolution occurs through increased levels of vibration (the actualization of your good deeds), through your higher levels of consciousness (your fruitful desires and thoughts), and through the refinement of your nervous system. This is the integration of soul, mind, and body in synchronistic unity. When issues arise where you would feel knocked down and wholly under stress, you no longer fret or cower. Instead, you go quietly within where your depth of stillness, creativity, and resolve reside and look for and receive answers. Herein are your strength and the source of your power, and the answers flow naturally. You do what is required to get through it and move on. In this way, you are developing your will, your courage, your power, and your resilience. From here onward, obstacles no longer faze you for you are in touch with pure potential. A feeling grows inside you that there is nothing you cannot get through, no matter how tough, for the toughness is only a façade; your struggles with life taper. You are at peace with yourself and the world.

Look inwardly to see if there are still deep desires to the material world. After all, it isn't easy to let go of things you have been holding on to for most of your life. That deep abyss of stillness and silence is within. Go there to reconcile anything that is difficult to overcome. You are affixed in the material world, but do what you must do through nonattachment. Nonattachment is the ability to be in an activity but feel complete separateness from the activity. It is the ability to move about and do what you need to do while remaining steadfastly in a state of detachment. I recall that I used to dislike washing dishes in the kitchen sink. But there came a time when my dishwasher was not functioning and I had no choice. At some point through this ordeal, I recognized stillness in and around me. I recognized that I was feeling at peace inside myself, feeling fulfilled and easy, empty of thoughts and very present. This was impossible, but it was happening. I felt everything more profoundly than ever before: the warmth and cuddling effects of the water as it meandered over my skin, my full recognition of the patterns and shapes being formed as the water passed over my hands, the fresh inviting scent of the dish soap touching my nostrils, the luster of the enamel plates and cups, and the sound of my voice in a delicate soft hum as I replicated a tune I loved. I caught myself in this moment of delight, of richness, of ecstasy. This was real. It felt completely alive. For a moment, it felt as if someone else were enjoying this experience, for it could not possibly have been me, but it was me.

Many other such moments have since occurred while I indulged in what would be considered mundane tasks. These moments stay inside your being like a recording that you can plug into and replay at any time. They are your subtle experiences, expressing to you, that bliss consciousness is rising in you. I prefer to call them "moments of bliss while standing firmly in your power". They come upon you quietly in moments of stillness, when you are at peace. Peace is the ground from which bliss and love arises. This is being present in the moment, and this is the soul rising.

Get a glimpse of your emerging soul as you play, sing, dance, perform mundane tasks, or take long walks in nature. Lose yourself in the present moment. Become everlastingly immersed in whatever you are doing, with your whole being and attention in the now. Do not criticize what you are doing as boring or tedious. Feel instead the emergence of the light as you become lost in the doing. And as you progress, every moment will begin to feel fresh and every activity brings a new appeal, a new discovery. As these moments of bliss come upon you, realize that you are experiencing the subtleties of spirit expanding in you, for you are stepping deeper into the light. The results of whatever activities you are doing will be done with absolute brilliance. Cherish these subtle moments, for your awareness is maturing and soul is burgeoning.

Be Rich with Purpose

To further liberate the soul, become imbued with giving, sharing, teaching, helping, volunteering, or any other verb that activates your nobility. Develop your altruistic radiance by serving others, and loving in every moment the doing of it. Make real the saying "Your talent is God's gift to you. What you do with it is your gift to God." "Where is God?" you may ask. Look directly into the eyes of everyone you serve and you will know, for in the giving and in the receiving, we are eternally bound to each other.

What are your passions, your qualities, and your strengths? Go inside to locate them. Describe them wholeheartedly, for they are also the passions, qualities, and strengths of the soul. They point to your abilities and your purpose here on earth, which are also perfectly aligned with your greatest desires, loves, passions, and God-given gifts. Everything you do from this point on must be rich with purpose, courage, and willpower, for you are becoming further grounded in spirit.

Now it's time to purge the things of nonsense that still bog your mind regularly, tying you with conviction to materialism on earth. As your level of consciousness increases, so does your wisdom. Wisdom allows your higher mind to become free to relinquish earthly egocentric desires and attitudes to which you may still be unconsciously bound. For example, you have longed for a particular vehicle and planned on purchasing one. Then one day you recognize that the desire is no longer there. It has simply vanished. Now you can examine other actions and desires you still hold, to verify their validity in your new higher life. You must choose to let go of the ones that are based on egocentric cravings or that have simply become irrelevant. This should be easy for you, for you created those desires with lower mind and now you are living from higher mind. The self you were previously has vanished and a new higher self has emerged. Your selfish actions are being replaced with selfless actions, and as your qualities of persistence and patience ensue, you are gaining mastery of the self and mental quietude. You are coming into alignment of oneness with your purpose. Your glow is shining through everything you think and everything you do, and it feels surreal yet real. The ego has been set aside. Feelings of peace and harmony with all others and all things are present in your energy field. The essence of love is bubbling inside you and the sense of oneness is growing in parallel. You are awakening to your true self.

Your thoughts and your actions carry weight. They are not separate from you and will come back to you in one form or another. Become aware, therefore, of the choices you make as often as you make them, for they create your personal truth that become your signature in the world. They create ripples in this lifetime and in lifetimes to come. Soul is your beacon and your guiding light. Build a bridge to the soul and create your heaven here on earth.

In his book *Life after Death*, Deepak Chopra states, "It's difficult for us to imagine being in the world but not of it, since our physical body is anchored in this world. But the soul manages to be in the world while remaining firmly outside time and space." The essence of your being is eternal. Be of courage and anchor yourself to your eternal nature. You have a physical body, but you are not your body. You are the essence of eternity that abides inside and outside the body and you will come to know this through subtle experiences arising from deeper levels of consciousness as you move deeper into the light.

Now how does your heaven on earth look to you? What legacy do you want to impart to humankind as you build that bridge to the soul? The answers lie within the soul. If you are aware of your soul's purpose here on earth in this particular lifetime, then you are ready to move forward. If you are unaware of your soul's desires or purpose, there are books that can assist you. I will enlist here a few suggestions that can help you to become familiar with the desires of the soul.

Suggestion 1

Get a pen and a notepad for this exercise. Now look back at your life in five-year increments, from the age of fifteen to twenty years and then from age twenty to twenty-five and so on, up to the age you are presently. Within each five-year increment, write down everything you can remember that was significant to you, for which you still have vivid memories and emotions; list the experiences that were both good and not good. When you have completed the exercise, look over each five-year increment and look for repetitive patterns, such as things that kept repeating themselves irrespective of the situation in which you were involved. Look for repetition of things you loved and things you did at different periods in your life, whether they came from negative or positive circumstances.

The desires of the soul are consistent and will keep repeating through your youth and into your adult life. These are things that you have repeated many times naturally but may not have recognized their significance, for at the time you knew not of soul or of the soul's desires. You were unaware that you came to this earthly plane with abilities for the benefit of humanity. Your gifts are the things you do that come effortlessly, naturally to you with joyous impact to others.

Suggestion 2

Sit in a meditative posture and still the mind. You are going into that sphere of silence from where everything comes. When the mind is still, mindfully ask, "What do I love to do so much, I would do it for free?" Wait for the answers.

Suggestion 3

Go for a walk in nature where you will not be interrupted. Nature has a way of touching the soul. Bring paper and pen. Sit comfortably in the grasp of Mother Nature, your bare feet firmly planted on the ground. Become still. Now examine your "natural abilities." This includes the things you do with little effort, yet the results are profound, as well as the things you have done repeatedly throughout your life that have assisted or uplifted others significantly. Whatever your talent, it is not something you spend ardent time cultivating. It comes to you as natural as breathing. When you have identified your gifts, look back over your life to see how often you used them, and recall their impact on others.

Suggestion 4

There are books on the market that claim to help people find their purpose.

Souls spend lifetimes honing and perfecting that which they love or are drawn to naturally. Your gifts therefore are not accidents. They are the loves of the soul actualized over countless lifetimes. When known, they can be used to significantly uplift life on earth. What do you think Whitney Houston spent lifetimes honing? What of six-year-old Emily Bear playing the piano since age three, wowing audiences and composing her own music? She's been dubbed as the next Mozart.

It has been said that whatever your purpose here on earth, you have unknowingly been doing it throughout your life but were completely unaware. Now bring your awareness to the forefront to examine the things you love to do that are effortless for you, and have the mark of brilliance, and have significantly helped others? What are your natural abilities for which you had no special training or education? What flows naturally from you? What do you do better than others who have had to zealously study or practice? What is it you are doing when you notice that time stands still? These are some clues to ascertain your loves. Some souls come here with multiple gifts to be exercised on earth, so examine all your natural abilities.

My loves and abilities in past lives included music, architecture, entrepreneurship, authorship, speaker/teacher, inventor, and problem solver. Those are also my natural abilities in this lifetime.

Higher mind, the soul, has an innate instinct to exercise the gifts that live within its field of influence, for it is bound to humanity as the branches are to the tree. The soul knows its duty to humanity and is imbued with the courage and the will to express it. Irrespective of the form in which it is expressed, it will always be in love and light, for any act of kindness touches the heart of everyone who bears witness. This is the nature of the soul for both the giver and the receiver. Now move to your calling. Do not procrastinate. Step farther into the light with courage. You are moving gracefully along the continuum.

During my years as an information technology technician in the corporate world, I became aware of my strong and natural abilities to improve and increase efficiency in things without much effort. I could see and understand what others could not. In that vein, I reengineered divisions of large corporations that significantly enhanced their business processes, improved their profit margin, and improved employee productivity twofold or threefold. In the process, I created comprehensive training programs for both technical and nontechnical staff. None of the above activities were part of my job description, but I exercised my abilities because they must be exercised to become mature, and to be of benefit to the receivers. In so doing, I qualified to myself my gifts, my abilities, and my willingness to serve.

Soul Ascension

Know that from the time you arrive on planet earth clothed in human form, you have been on a spiritual journey. It could not be any other way since you are spirit. You have been unaware of who you are, where you come from, and the reasons for which you incarnated here on earth. Through your heightened awareness, you have come to know that you are soul and that you have a specific purpose here on earth, which is to return to your true self as a spark of divine light. You have become aware that to reach this goal, you must significantly advance your awareness to higher energy frequencies, to evolve the soul. You must become aligned with the purpose of the soul and live in the higher energies of the evolved soul. To grow into what is soul at its core includes compassion, love, harmony, peace, and bliss. Where are you right now? Are you in alignment, out of alignment, or are you moving into alignment with soul?

A time may come, through the grace of God, when you will receive an anointing that is the ascension of the soul, which is a move to higher levels of consciousness. There is nothing that you can do to cause this anointing to occur. You have been preparing yourself by becoming aligned with your higher self, which has taken you to higher levels of awareness from where you previously stood. This anointing is soul ascension—ascending the soul to higher frequencies. Some also call this enlightenment or spiritual awakening. Spiritual ascension is the liberation of the soul and is possible only for souls that have progressed sufficiently in awareness and understanding. This will bring about a significant shift to higher dimensions to which you will have access, significantly elevating your level of awareness.

Do you wish to know what higher frequencies are, and what their relationship to spiritual advancement is? We are infinite beings, and the universe is infinite. Infinity has no beginning and no end. It is limitless. When you are willing to perceive outside of your immediate scope, the possibilities of accessing other dimensions become endless. In this limitless universe, there is a vastness of energy that organizes itself in bands of frequencies: the farther apart the bands (vibrations), the more different the energy frequency. Inside each band of frequency are distinct "world" dimensions, each one being very different from the next. Each band vibrates at a different energy frequency from the next and provides vastly different spectrums of experiences. Your level of awareness is also energy. If you are willing to do the work to increase your spiritual vibration, thus increasing your awareness, you will have access to higher energy frequencies that match your level of awareness, possibly in the same dimension or in higher dimensions. Your experiences, therefore, will be aligned with your level of awareness.

As you further elevate your energy through the practice of consistently heightening your spiritual vibration, many more worlds/dimensions will be opened up to you and the possibilities and realities inside those worlds are endless.

The process of soul ascension is your energy and awareness becoming elevated into new worlds of perception, experience, and creation. You are moving from one layer to the next, with broader experiences to be had. You can ascend within a dimensional reality (world) as well as between dimensions. You elevate your energy, awaken your awareness, and experience a new world. That new world is both what you experience (inside) and the outer realities you brought back from the experiences.

Each time you move higher in awareness, it is yet another beginning of realization of the next possibility, the next world of awareness.

The process of ascension comes on suddenly and can be a bit perplexing at first, until you realize that you are being freed of your baggage. The term used for this rapture is "the dark night of the soul," and it can occur just before bedtime or as you are coming out of sleep in the morning, although there is no rule for its arrival.

In a previous chapter, I spoke of going inside and asking your higher self to bring forth your subconscious wounds so you can process them and let them go. During the "dark night" process, all of your subconscious wounds, your unprocessed emotions and old traumas, your karma, your distorted beliefs, and other dark energies that rest in your chakras, will rise to the surface to be processed in the now. It is important that you shine the light of your conscious awareness on each dark energy as it emerges. Feel the emotions without creating or recalling your story around them. See them and feel them. Look for the wisdom inherent in each situation as it emerges, because all traumatic experiences have lessons to be learned. Look at the part you played in the trauma and take acceptance of it. Become keenly conscious of the wisdom being imparted to you through each experience. Allow each experience and its memory to move through you. Then let it go in love and light. These dark energies will move through your chakra system and out of your body, both physically and subtly. Do not resist the feelings that come up during this process, or else you will create new blockages restricting your ascension.

The baggage you are releasing is dark energy, and since energy cannot be destroyed, it must be transmuted from lower frequency to higher frequency or into light. Imagine the dark energies being released as murky dark shadows, and as you release them, imagine them being transmuted into a golden platinum light—the light of "the Christ consciousness." This is energy transmuting from lower to higher frequency. See the dark energies being enveloped by the golden light. Now ask the divine to send the golden platinum light into and around all your bodies: your physical and all your subtle (spirit) bodies. Imagine the light surrounding all your bodies and bask in the beauty and lightness that comes from the divine light. Now you are free. *Sat chit ananda.*

Although the ascension process can be overwhelming, even a bit frightening, you must become aware of what is happening, or else you may lose the opportunity to properly rid yourself of all your stored baggage. If you do this work with good effort, your wounds will be released permanently from your energy system. This includes the release of your karma and the further demise of the ego. This is a significant shift from lower consciousness to higher levels of consciousness and awareness. You may feel lost, displaced, anxious, empty, and very alone. This is because the old unproductive energies that occupied your energy field, the ones with which you unconsciously identified yourself, have been lifted and removed. You are no longer the person you were yesterday. Who are you now? You are uncertain, for all you have been and known is suddenly no longer present. Like a newborn moving through the birth canal, it is quite uncomfortable. It may take you some time to adjust to your new environment, which is your elevated energy and deeper awareness into higher dimensions and higher energy frequencies. You are now on a higher level of consciousness.

This process may occur several times during your spiritual growth and transformation, and with each occurrence, your energy and awareness will move higher into new worlds of insight, experiences, and growth. This is the significant progress every person on the spiritual walk yearns for. Impart your newfound wisdom to other souls as you live in the purity of love.

Raise Your Frequency

So how do you prepare yourself for soul ascension? How do you raise your level of awareness to ready yourself for ascension or to integrate to higher energy frequency?

You do it through incorporating your soul into everything you do, everything you say, how you think, how you treat others, your reaction or interpretations to what happens, and most profoundly, that you love. Love yourself, and express love to others. When you can do this, you will be aligning yourself with the soul, which will raise your level of vibration.

Love is a quality of the soul. You need not look far, for you are the purity of love in your naturalness. When you are still, it is love that emanates from your being. But where is love when your mind is racing? Most days you perceive good and bad from others and from situations. You are challenged with things that are difficult and this weighs on you; you don't feel love anywhere, for you are in a chaotic mind. When mind is running the show, everything loving is overshadowed by chaos. What resonates with most people on a daily basis is some form of strife, whether light or heavy, and that is where your energy lies, in chaos. This roller coaster with mind is not your natural state, for it has no flavoring of your essence. Come to notice the moments in which you have given control back to ego, when you are outside your essence. Now take a moment to get back into the self. Become still and recognize the play of duality where you swing back and forth between ego and your spiritual essence. You must further develop self-mastery. That means opening your mind's eye to seeing the cosmic perfection behind all events being played out before you. When you do this, there is no judgment, only understanding and wisdom.

What would you do to increase the capacity of love within you? Whatever comes up, do it. Express love to others. What you exercise flourishes, becomes stronger, and you become wholly capable of maturing your outward display of love. Since love is the nature of everyone, then others will feel that love when it is displayed to them. And the love inside them will grow to be expressed outwardly. Love begets more love.

Go into a place where the homeless are being fed and just watch. Watch the humility on the faces of those serving. Watch the humbleness and gratitude on the faces of those being served. Now what are you feeling? Notice that when you gaze upon kindness and generosity, love emerges in you. It just shows up. When one becomes selfless; can observe without judgment; is at peace with whatever happens; sees the good in all situations; can remain in a place of peace; then one is living from ultimate truth. That is love, peace, and bliss. Embracing and expressing love will increase your vibration.

Create peace from within by utilizing the system of the soul. Look back at past events where you passed judgment on yourself and on others and re-contextualize the situation by looking through the eyes of soul. Soul is the grandest version of the vision you hold about who you are. The soul's perspective is unique to the soul, for soul transcends the perspective of mind and holds a panoramic view of life as it unfolds. Let's examine an event through simple mind and then through the mind of soul. In this example, I will use the three brands of truth as outlined by Neil Donald Walsh: imagined, apparent, and actual.

Situation: a married couple cannot get along.

Three Brands of Truth

- imagined
  Wife: "He is sloppy and uneducated and knows not of reason."
  Husband: "She is a liar and lied about everything."
- apparent
  They are getting a divorce.
- actual (soul)
  The two parties co-created the experience for their souls' agenda.

The soul's perspective will always be one in which there is no finger-pointing. It will always be one in which you can look back at the situation and extract the wisdom of the experience. Souls come together to create experiences for the learning of both parties. Look through the mind of soul to allocate the wisdom being imparted to you.

Look back and examine the things that still disturb you about past experiences, but this time, look through the eyes of the soul. The soul has the wisdom of the ages and knows the orchestration of the life you are seeking. Lower mind cannot see at this depth and knows only to point the finger at others. Once you see things from the soul's perspective, wisdom will flourish in you and you will realize that there is no blame to be cast and no fingers to be pointed. Abide in the experiences that life provides for you. Search feverishly for the wisdom within each experience. Remember simple mind is limited, for it cannot access eternal data. Soul is metaphysical and has access to all there is; therefore, use the soul's data to expand the data of the mind. Thus, the actual truth you hold about an event can be elevated in the mind. This will help the mind to understand what the soul already knows. Progress along these lines will increase the capacity of the mind that will invariably raise your spiritual vibration.

Recognize that you are spirit carrying around a human body. Dispel the thought that you are human with spirit inside you. You are the aliveness and the electricity that brings life and movement and all else into this dense human body. Spirit has a vastly higher level of frequency than the human body. Your knowing that you are spirit will elevate you to higher levels of awareness. Build a relationship with yourself, which is spirit. Speak to your higher self when you need answers and know that he or she will respond. Connect with spirit through meditation and ask for guidance. Be still and allow the power of spirit, which is peace, love, joy, and contentment, to seep into who you become, for these are divine attributes that will filter into your consciousness and heighten your awareness. When you *know* without a doubt that you are spirit, you will shift to higher awareness.

Secure yourself in arenas of higher vibration. Negative situations or environments cause you to lapse into negative frequencies. This also means that the vibration of other people will dim your frequency or will adversely affect you. When you feel negative vibrations, move away from them. What are the things that bring you to feelings of complete peace or joy? Become involved in them as much as possible and feel the rhythm of heightened vibrations filtering through and around you. Spend time in nature. It naturally feels good. It is relaxing, soothing, comforting, and resonates a high frequency of love, innocence, and simplicity. Nature possesses absolute beauty and its energies have healing power. The body and soul are naturally drawn to positive things. Come to notice when you feel strong positive energy, and stay with it. And when you are feeling strong negative energy, do not spend your time in it. Simply exit to stage left.

Determine the things that motivate you and indulge feverishly in them to raise your vibration frequently. Through meditation, slip into the void and feel bliss. Stay there for a while to immerse yourself in the vibration. Create powerful emotions by doing things that inspire you deeply. Listen to music that causes you to move, to dance, no matter who is watching. Share your kindness with others by helping them out of their despair. Constantly monitor your own vibration, and when it feels low, do the things you love to move it to higher frequencies. Become wholly responsible for honing your spiritual self to higher vibrations. There is a vastness of experience out there waiting for you to indulge in.

Be of the highest integrity. Do not lie. Tell the truth about yourself to yourself. Tell the truth about yourself to others. Tell the truth about others to them, but soothe your words with kindness. Look through the mind of the soul and see things as they are, devoid of perception. Then there is no illusion, no negativity, no jealousy, no anger, and no disgust. Look toward the wisdom that you have gained. Rely upon it for it is knowledge, right knowledge, and it is the right way of knowing. It is infinite, it comes from within, and it is the nature of the soul. This knowing will dissolve the ego. Build your character upon fruitful behaviors and habits and treat others as if you see the divine in them, and one day you will. This will raise your spiritual vibration.

Share who you are, as you evolve. As each evolutionary stage is realized, from loss of mental limitations; shifting to higher frequencies; moving toward cosmic consciousness; and moving toward enlightenment; all pain and suffering disappears. You are able to experience your own true self, which is a proliferation in spiritual growth. Shine your light brightly into the world. Become an inspiration to others by sharing who you have become, so that they can see and know the salvation that awaits them. Speak, write, and counsel, for you see rightly and your tongue delivers what is in your heart. Do what is spiritually beneficial for humanity to create more radiant beings on planet earth. Namaste.

Your body is the temple of the soul, and it too vibrates. It is yours to take tremendous care of. Keep it in an optimum state, free from stresses; from repeated emotional challenges; from pollutants; and from edible substances of low frequency. A healthy body vibrates at a frequency of 62-78 MHz. When this frequency drops, the immune system is compromised. Many pollutants lower your healthy frequency, as do processed foods, canned foods, and GMO foods, which all have a frequency of zero. In general, foods of lower frequencies will cause your body's frequency to drop.

Now imagine what foods with zero frequency will do to your body. In fact, we will refer to these as "nonfood" since they are manmade and, therefore, not real. Fresh produce, that is organically grown, measures 20–27 MHz, fresh herbs measure 20–27 MHz, and dried herbs measure 12–22 MHz. According to Dr. Royal R. Rife, every disease has a frequency. He found that certain frequencies could prevent the development of disease and, in some cases, destroy lower-frequency diseases. Therefore, we need to keep our body frequency at its optimum state with the right substances that are compatible on a cellular/energy level. The body's frequency will drop so low that it becomes a host for microscopic invaders. Disease in the body starts when your vibration drops to 58 MHz. Receptivity to cancer starts at 42 MHz, and death begins at 25 MHz. Therefore, whatever you digest, ensure it is within the higher-frequency foods to protect yourself. Be healthy and be good. Namaste.

The chart below is an energy-frequency food-vibration chart that will assist you in choosing what to eat. It goes from highest to lowest frequency.

Please note that this is a guide and it is best to consult with a naturopathic doctor or nutritionist who can guide you on what is best for your body type. For example, if you need to eat meat protein, there are many farmers who are raising free-range livestock without antibiotics or hormones. The same goes for dairy. Read the labels to ensure that your yogurt or milk is organic, with natural enzymes intact. These enzymes are crucial to a healthy gut. There is evidence that most diseases start in an unhealthy stomach.

The most important thing to remember is balance. Make sure that you have a well-balanced diet that is in complete harmony with your body. Make sure that what you eat is primarily natural and of good quality.

Energy-Frequency Food-Vibration Chart

Highest

- essential oils
- fresh herbs
- dried herbs
- fresh vegetables
- fruits
- living grains
- legumes
- nuts

Medium

- dairy
- fish (non-bottom-feeders)
- chicken, other fowl
- eggs

Lowest

- red-meat, pork
- game meat
- fish (bottom-feeders)
- scavengers (crustaceans)

References

Chopra, Deepak; Life After Death: the burden of proof; 1st ed; New York, Harmony Books; 2006

McAdams, Dan P; The Redemptive Self: Stories Americans Live By; Revised and Expanded edition oxford university press; 2013 OCTOBER 2011 Newsletter Content

Tolle, Eckhart; Dark Night of the Soul; www.eckharttolle.com/newsletter; Eckhart Teachings Inc.; October-2011

Minero, Luis; Demystifying The Out Of Body Experiences: A Practical Manual for Exploration and Personal Evolution; 1st edition; Llewellyn Publications; 2012

Krishnamurti, Jiddu; The Urgency Of Change; 1st ed; Harper Collins 1970

Printed in the United States
By Bookmasters